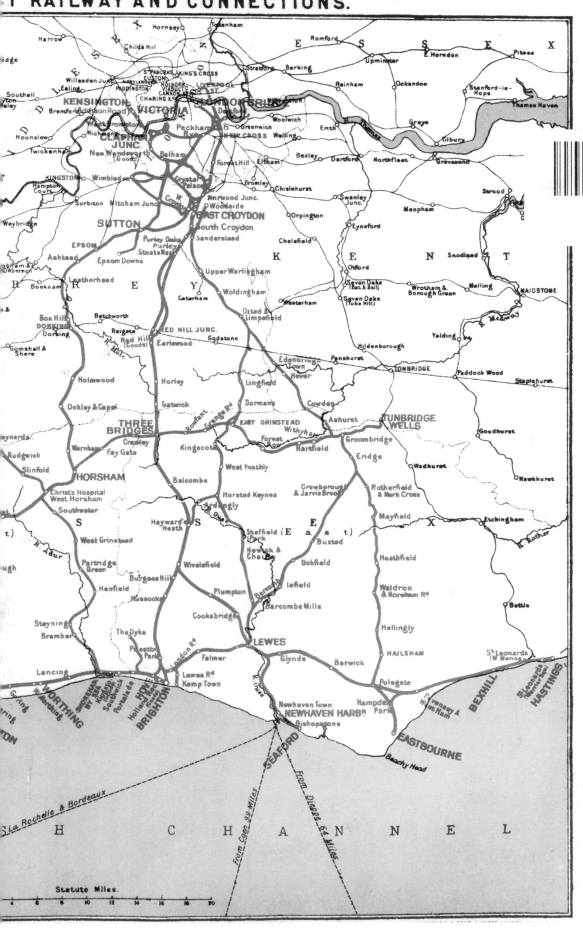

LONDON, BRIGHTON & SOUTH COAST RAILWAY
MISCELLANY

The cavernous interior of Brighton Central with two 'D1' tanks and a 'B4' visible. The double-sided platform was for ease of loading and unloading, although weighed against this was the space it occupied. Notice the centre engine release and storage roads, a common feature during steam days. *IAL*

LONDON, BRIGHTON & SOUTH COAST RAILWAY
MISCELLANY

Kevin Robertson

OPC

An imprint of
Ian Allan Publishing

Contents

It is Derby Day 1874 and a succession of trains for race-goers has resulted in this scene of waiting locomotives at Epsom Downs, among them Craven and Stroudley designs. Incidentally, the 1874 race winner was named 'George Frederick', ridden by H. Custance and trained by Tom Leader. No doubt its owner, Mr Cartwright, was well satisfied! *IAL*

Acknowledgements and Bibliography

In producing this Miscellany, I am deeply indebted to Brian Arman, Eric Best, R. C. 'Dick' Riley and Denis Tillman.

The following works have also been consulted in full or part:

Locomotives of the LBSCR, D. L. Bradley (RCTS)
The Southern Railway, C. F. Dendy-Marshall (Ian Allan Publishing)
London's Elevated Electric Railway, G. Goslin (Conner & Butler)
The London, Brighton & South Coast Railway, C. Hamilton Ellis (Ian Allan Publishing)
The London, Brighton & South Coast Railway, J. Howard-Turner (Batsford)
Brighton Line Album, R. C. Riley (Ian Allan Publishing)

First published in 2004

ISBN 0 86093 583 3

Published by Oxford Publishing Co

an imprint of Ian Allan Publishing Ltd, Hersham, Surrey KT12 4RG.
Printed by Ian Allan Publishing Ltd, Hersham, Surrey KT12 4RG.

Code: 0404/A2

Title page:
Departure from Victoria in the days of steam and mechanical signalling: Atlantic No 41, later *Peveril Point*, heads what is probably one of the prestige Brighton services. Together with sister engine No 40 — by then No 2040 — these two were the first of the former LBSCR 4-4-2s to be withdrawn in early 1944; No 41 was destined to be cut up at Eastleigh works. *IAL*

Introduction

It is more than 80 years since the LBSCR was swallowed up into the then conglomerate of the Southern Railway — 80 years in which subsequent owners and operators have attempted to obliterate almost all but the fixed infrastructure of what was once one of the great railway companies of the kingdom. The origins of the line may be traced back as far as 1823 with the first published proposals for 'rail-road' communication between 'The Metropolis' and the ports of Shoreham (Brighton), Rochester (Chatham) and Portsmouth. This scheme was in fact the title of a grand plan by one William James, albeit one that came to nothing, as did an equally bold 1825 proposal for a London to Bristol via Brighton line. England was perhaps not ready for 'rail-roads' away from the North at this time, but the moment was soon approaching when it would be, and that time came in 1837 with the passing of the 'London to Brighton Railway' Act, authorising construction of what would become the main line to the South Coast, together with branches to Shoreham and Newhaven, via Lewes.

Thus 'from little acorns' did the railway system develop, although it should be said at this stage that the London & Brighton Railway's section from Brighton to Shoreham actually opened in 1840, more than a year before the main line south from London, locomotives to operate the service having to be delivered by sea! In keeping with the aspirations of the directors, in 1846 the name was changed to the London, Brighton & South Coast Railway following amalgamation with the London & Croydon Railway, and soon afterwards the first extension from the original prospectus was made westward from Brighton to Chichester in 1847, and to Portsmouth a little later in the same year. This was followed in the next few years by extensions from Horsham to Three Bridges (1848), Pulborough and Petworth (1859), Steyning and Shoreham (1861), Littlehampton (1863), Bognor (1864), and Dorking and Leatherhead (1867). There had also been expansion within the London area, involving what were fast becoming the popular residential areas of Camberwell, Lambeth, Croydon, Banstead, Epsom Downs and Tooting.

Accordingly, by 1869 the route mileage of the company was already 365, with a gross revenue of some £709,654 recorded for the half-year ended 31 December 1868. The

This is Honor Oak Park, looking south *circa* 1911, with No 623 — renumbered as such in 1908 — on an up train. Originally named *Mayfield*, it lost its name in 1905. *IAL*

balance-sheet for the time also reveals a healthy situation with an authorised share capital of £18.6 million, of which £600,000 had not been called upon.

A similar situation would continue through to the end of the Victorian era, when the development of the electric tramway began to make serious inroads into profits, particularly within the London area, with the result that the company was forced to act. The result was the famous overhead electrification brought into use in 1909 and eventually expanded right up to 1923 and beyond. That the electrification was a success is not in doubt; indeed, its very success was also to be its downfall, with overcrowding becoming a common feature — the same criticism was levelled decades later. The use of catenary was particularly interesting, as for general suburban work the exposed third rail had up to then been recognised as perfectly suitable. Overhead electrification was, however, regarded as preferable where longer distances were involved, so did the directors have in mind the eventual electrification of the main line through to the coast? Probably the answer is yes, although history would intervene to prevent this, and it would not be until almost 20 years later that the Southern Railway, as successor to the LBSCR, would complete the electrification of the main line, albeit with a third rail; the same system is still in use today.

The inference, therefore, is that both the public and the board were far from satisfied with the available performance of the steam engines of the period. However, that is unlikely to be true, as the engines of the LBSCR were no worse than those of any other railway company. While the single-wheelers that still survived were often blamed for causing delays, in truth the real reason was the excessive loads they were now required to haul, far above the original specification set down years earlier. Indeed, steam had proven its worth many times over, perhaps one of the most memorable occasions being on 26 July 1903 when, as an experiment to see if it would be possible to replicate the suggested potential electric timing over the 51 miles from London to Brighton, runs of 48 minutes were achieved in the down direction and 50 minutes in the up. The load was four vehicles, and a maximum speed of 90mph was attained on the down service.

Shades, then, of Gresley who, years later, perhaps failed to recognise that steam could only achieve such efforts with a willing crew and an engine in exemplary condition. Other difficulties arose on congested routes where it was far from easy to keep a section of track clear for a limited number of high-speed workings while still dovetailing in the rest of the service. Again, shades of both BR and the present privatised operators.

To operate the system one of the principal requirements was an adequate supply of motive power and rolling stock, and it may be appropriate to introduce here perhaps the most famous of all the LBSCR Locomotive Engineers, William Stroudley. The choice of Stroudley as Engineer was maybe strange, to say the least. Taking up the post in 1870, his previous roles had been as Works Manager in the Cowlairs shops of the Edinburgh & Glasgow Railway, then as Locomotive Superintendent of the Highland Railway, neither of which had given him much opportunity to prove his abilities.

None the less, the LBSCR had made a wise choice, and Stroudley brought with him simple ideas that would serve the railway well past his own death in December 1889. These ideas involved little rebuilding of previous designs, which in itself was somewhat unusual, as most new engineers invariably attempted to improve on the work of their predecessors. Instead, he simply allowed the older designs to 'work themselves out', and to replace them he produced only half a dozen or so classes of new design, renowned for their originality, neatness and common interchangeability of parts. Included among these were the famous 'Terrier' tanks, originally intended for working on the East London Railway and the South London line between Victoria and London Bridge.

It is unlikely that any enthusiasts, regardless of their personal preferences, will fail to acknowledge the 'Terriers' as a masterpiece. This is even more creditable when one considers that they were a pinnacle of locomotive design from the late Victorian era. A fact not widely known about the design is that eight engines of identical type were built in 1875 in Australia for use on the New South Wales Government Railway (the subsequent fate of these engines is not known).

The 'Terriers' would also not remain solely on the LBSCR, and examples were subsequently to migrate to the neighbouring South Eastern & Chatham, London & South Western, and Isle of Wight lines. Later still other examples would be sold to other bodies, including the Newhaven Harbour Company and the Weston, Clevedon & Portishead Railway, the latter being eventually absorbed by the GWR, as well as into industrial use.

The LBSCR practice of naming engines after local placenames also reached its peak under Stroudley. However, with so many engines it became necessary to choose locations away from the area served by the railway; interestingly, there is no record of any passengers complaining that they had been confused by the name borne by a particular engine and had arrived at the wrong destination (the excuse used by the GWR some years later to justify the removal of names from several of its engines)!

Following on from the 'Terriers' came the 'D' tanks, an 0-4-2T type, and shortly afterwards the 0-6-0T 'E' class design. Coincident with the development of the various tank engines was the introduction of the first of the singles, the initial engine appearing with 6ft 9in driving wheels, subsequently reduced to 6ft 6in for the remainder of the class. Unlike other designers, who were perhaps too proud to admit when change was needed, Stroudley was shrewd enough to recognise where improvement could be made, and as successive engines were built he also reduced the cylinder diameter, until arriving at an optimum 16in by 22in for the type.

The ability of the single-wheelers to haul ever-increasing train weights was, of course, limited by the adhesive ability of just a single pair of driving wheels, so it comes as no surprise that the next development was for a class of 0-4-2 tender engines, this time with 5ft 6in wheels. This was

An unidentified 'B1' is on the four-track section near Balham, destined for the South Coast, complete with two Pullman vehicles among the formation. Clearly re-sleepering has recently taken place, and while the lineside is reasonably tidy, the same cannot be said for the actual permanent way, which must be somewhat unusual for the period. *IAL*

followed by a series having the same basic wheel arrangement, but with a driving wheel diameter increased to 6ft 6in. Despite murmurings that the larger leading wheels would surely cause derailments, such premonitions of doom were unfounded and the success of the type quickly led to the remarkable 'Gladstones', surely the tender equivalent of the success achieved by the 'Terriers'. However, despite several 'Terriers' having survived, only one Stroudley tender engine remains, 'B' class No 214 *Gladstone* itself. Thirty-six were built, the last 10 appearing after the death of the designer.

As well as engines for passenger work, Stroudley also designed the 'C' class 0-6-0 goods engines. Twelve were built between 1882 and 1887, and served the freight needs of the company well. The only surprise perhaps is that more were not built.

Stroudley was very much of the opinion that individual engines should be allocated to dedicated drivers, for in this way far better reliability was derived from both. He got his way during his tenure, but this was a time when labour was both cheap and plentiful, and such ideals could not apply in later decades; it is interesting to imagine how Stroudley would have reacted to the changing motive power needs of the 1930s and 1940s.

Following on from Stroudley was Robert J. Billinton, who migrated from the Midland Railway at Derby. Under his custodianship larger designs would appear, and while perhaps some of the finery of the Stroudley era was abandoned, this could not be said of the finish applied to the engines of the period as far as their paintwork and cleanliness were concerned.

Billinton's time on the Midland had convinced him of the desirability of applying a trailing bogie to the basic tank engine design wherever possible, and accordingly his first design, the 'D3' type, followed this concept. (Some engines of Stroudley's 'E' class were completed during the start of his tenure, but the 'D3s' were Billinton's first actual design.) Larger tank engines followed a more conventional pattern, and with the 0-6-2T 'E3s' there would be no copy of the Midland 'Flatirons' which were 0-6-4Ts! As train weights increased and technology developed, the next stage in development was a 4-4-0 tender engine: first came the 'B2' class, closely followed by the 'B4', which was overall a most impressive design, having 6ft 9in driving wheels and wonderful curved splashers over the bogie wheels. These engines were introduced between 1899 and 1902, and carried names in keeping with the penchant of the period for

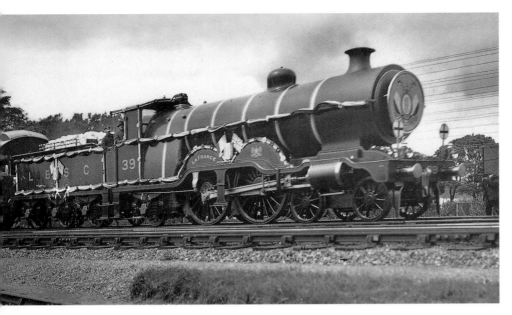

On 24 June 1913 No 39 *La France*, appropriately, is decorated for the official visit of the new French President, Monsieur Raymond Poincaré, taking him from Portsmouth to Victoria. The bunting is already showing signs of wanting to detach itself from the handrail, while the whitewashed coal is an interesting addition! *IAL*

taking pride in both the Empire and its citizens: *Canada, Queensland, Cecil Rhodes, Empress* and *Balmoral* are some classic examples.

But such splendour came at a price, and as far as maintenance was concerned there were already calls for economy. Accordingly, in 1902 experiments commenced in the use of oil as a fuel, but as others would find in later years, any advantage was perhaps nominal and coal would remain the preferred choice for the remainder of the life of the company. Further tank engines of the 'E5' and 'E6' classes followed in 1904/5, the latter design never seen by its designer beyond the drawing-board, as he died 'in harness' in November 1904.

The next man at the head of the Locomotive Department was Douglas Earle Marsh. An engineer of great experience, his earlier career had been spent at both Swindon and Doncaster, and it was from the post of assistant to Ivatt on the Great Northern Railway that he arrived at Brighton in January 1905. Marsh's ideas were to prove radical to some, but logical to others. One of his first steps was to alter the locomotive livery to a dark umber in place of yellow, and also to adopt a black livery for goods classes. Most names were also abolished.

As far as his first designs were concerned, there was an equally radical approach. Two steam railcars were introduced, together with two petrol railcars. However, a generally more successful approach to cost-cutting was the development of the motor-train principle, in which the LBSCR led the way with its use of air for both control and braking. As regards Marsh's general engineering prowess, to the enthusiast the LBSCR's success has perhaps long been overshadowed by Drummond on the neighbouring London & South Western Railway. This is partly due to the impact of Drummond's personality: he was known to have been an extremely fiery and strong-willed character. However, Marsh enjoyed success after success. His operation of the motor-trains was followed by his magnificent Atlantic designs, which became the 'H1' and 'H2' classes. These set new standards in speed and reliability on the main line from

London, and would not be bettered until the introduction of electrification decades later.

What could well have been Marsh's crowning glory perhaps fell somewhat short of expectations. The first two 4-4-2T classes quickly became hated due to their limited steaming abilities, although there was some improvement when, thanks to the aid of his Chief Draughtsman, B. K. Field, superheating was introduced later on. The idea behind the introduction of these tank engines was none the less well thought out. On a system where the longest nonstop run was only just in excess of 60 miles, it made sense to use tank engines, while the 'H1' and 'H2' classes were kept back for the very best workings — an example was the use of temporarily named 'H1' *La France* for the visit of the French President in 1913.

A pair of still larger tank engines appeared in 1910, with a 4-6-2T wheel arrangement. Although the two locomotives were externally similar, the valve gear differed on each engine, and with only two being constructed it is reasonable to assume that they were intended to be the guinea pigs for the subsequent development of similar engines. In the event this was not to be: Marsh's retirement and the advent of war put paid to any desire to develop further types of express engine for the duration.

The new man in charge, from January 1912, was L. B. Billinton. The son of R. J. Billinton, he had worked for the LBSCR from an early age, slowly progressing through the department, which meant that he was well versed in both the history and requirements of the system. Offset against this, however, was his lack of outside experience, which might have been expected to lead to the continuation of past practice without thought for utilising ideas from elsewhere.

In fact, L. B. Billinton was to prove a colossus of an engineer. His 'K' class 2-6-0 goods engine appeared in 1913, and placed the LBSCR head and shoulders above its neighbours as far as goods designs were concerned for almost 30 years. What an opportunity was missed to multiply the type in future years, although, as would occur later, it was invariably down to the background of the later CME of the

Southern Railway after the Grouping in 1923, Maunsell, and his own personal preferences, as well as the charisma of his staff, that would lead to development in the future. More on this theme anon.

Billinton's second and final design for the LBSCR was the massive 4-6-4T 'L' class tank engine, of which seven were built, the first in 1914 and the remainder in 1921/2. This was the logical development of Marsh's 4-6-2T class of a few years earlier, and the locomotives would prove eminently successful in their allotted task until rebuilt as tender engines in the 1930s. This later rebuilding was not in any way due to any fault in design. The reasons for doing it were twofold. First was the Southern Railway's antipathy — understandable, though hardly excusable — to the use of large tank engines on fast passenger trains, and second there was a recognition that the basic design could still play a useful role as a steam type for some years to come as electrification progressed. Indeed, that was certainly the case, and the rebuilt class later ventured far afield from its original haunts.

As far as mechanical engineering was concerned, the grouping of the three South Coast railways into the Southern Railway resulted in the ideals of both Ashford (SECR) and Eastleigh (LSWR) dominating the group. Maunsell, the new chief, was a former SECR man who had shrewdly noticed the success of the use of large tank engines on the neighbouring line, resulting in his introduction of the 'River' tank design of similar wheel arrangement, but utilising his standard 'Ashford' parts. However, the disastrous Sevenoaks derailment meant an end to the use of tank engines, although the cause was arguably more to do with civil engineering than the locomotive.

With the Chief Mechanical Engineer's department also now centred on Eastleigh, it is not surprising that the influence of LSWR designers Urie and Drummond was paramount, and while there can be little doubt that the products of Brighton were well worth considering for future development, events would decree otherwise. It would take a different era and a different form of transport to prove such ideals of the LBSCR as the use of air brakes and overhead electrification were in fact preferable to the practices perpetuated by its neighbours.

On the civil engineering side, one of the first plans for a terminus for trains within London was for the embryo London & Brighton line to share the existing facility of the London & Southampton line at Nine Elms. Fortunately, perhaps, for both parties, this was not proceeded with and, instead, the terminus at London Bridge, was preferred. A number of what today would be considered hare-brained suggestions were made in connection with the new railway, though no doubt seriously intended at the time. One of these was the scheme of one John S. Vallance, whose idea for almost any railway was to link the destinations by tunnel and blow or suck trains through the whole length — known as an 'atmospheric railway'. Others suggested similar schemes, which were of course wholly in keeping with the general contemporary belief that atmospheric propulsion was a major contender. The London & Croydon Railway, which was

amalgamated with the London & Brighton in 1847 to form the LBSCR, had experimented briefly with atmospheric propulsion earlier in that year. In the end, however, a locomotive-operated system was preferred for the LBSCR.

In the event an overland route was constructed, running almost due south from the metropolis, dissecting en route the chalk ridge of the South Downs. Throughout there were five tunnels, of a total length exceeding 3⅓ miles, the longest of which, at 2,259yd, was Clayton Tunnel. Contemporary records report that the tunnels were whitewashed throughout, and were also lit by gas '…which, though not of much value to the passenger (though, in him, it induces a feeling of confidence and cheerfulness), is to the engine driver of utmost moment, enabling him to see the road throughout as well almost as in broad day…' It was none the less no doubt also intended to reassure passengers, who would otherwise be unaccustomed to travel through what was then deemed the bowels of the earth.

The serious side of illuminating tunnels was of course to assist the driver in observing any obstruction ahead at a time when both signals and braking were rudimentary in the extreme. Whether any genuine assistance could be gained in gas lighting is perhaps doubtful, for the smoke from the locomotive would tend to negate any advantage, while an 1861 accident in Clayton Tunnel, at a time when a form of signalling was already in use, proved that a careful lookout was perhaps paramount.

Signalling itself had been used from almost the earliest days, albeit in rudimentary form. As time passed, so the development of the electric telegraph and interlocking assisted in ensuring safety, although in reality the vigilance of staff also played a great part. As an example, one might do well to quote Sir Frederick Smith on behalf of the Board of Trade, who in 1841 referred to some 150-200 trains daily passing through Greenwich Junction without the slightest incident. His opinion was that the selection of good men and good administration was the best safeguard rather than 'the introduction of new mechanical appliances'.

No doubt due to the heavy engineering required, the cost of construction of the original main line was in the order of £40,000 per mile, or some £2 million for the whole route. This included what can only be described as the magnificent Ouse Valley viaduct, 1,475ft in length and comprising 37 30ft arches having a maximum height of 96ft. It remains in use today, although the achievement in building it at a time when muscle-power, both human and equine, was almost all that was available to the early engineers, is nowadays mostly forgotten.

Of course, one of the published advantages to gain support for the new railways generally was a reduction in travel time between destinations, although this can hardly have been the case in 1844, when it was reported that an excursion from London had taken some 4½ hours to reach the coast, an average speed of just over 13mph.

Another necessary feat of engineering, also illustrated in this book, was the swingbridge at Ford. This was at first hand-operated, according to a contemporary report opened by '…two men and a boy … in about five minutes. The

Most famous of all the viaducts on the original London to Brighton line must be that across the Ouse Valley, designed by J. U. Rastrick and illustrated here shortly after completion. *Author's collection*

operation being undertaken by toothed wheels and racks and wrought iron winches.' This bridge was the scene of a macabre incident in 1851 when a passenger train ran into the rear of a cattle train. The driver of the latter jumped into the river to save himself, while the other driver, who had been at fault for disregarding a signal, attempted to slit his own throat as recognition of his guilt; he failed, so he too jumped into the river. He was rescued, presumably none too willingly, by a guard, but his subsequent fate is not recorded.

On the line itself two other accidents of interest are worth recording. The first occurred in October 1841 when a double-headed train became derailed in a cutting just north of Haywards Heath. The cause was put down to the weight of the train travelling at too fast a speed — 30mph — on what was newly laid track, although some controversy ensued over the merits of the type of engine involved. The second was between Falmer and Lewes in 1851, the result of vandalism. A local youth was suspected of placing a sleeper across the track, which resulted in the death of five persons, including the driver and fireman, although it could not be proved at the time that the youth was indeed the culprit.

A few years later, in 1859, occurred a boiler explosion. This was by no means uncommon in the early years of railways, often due to the engineers of the day failing to recognise the deterioration that could occur in fireboxes and boilers, while drivers had been known to screw down safety valves in an attempt to secure increased power from their often grossly overloaded engines. In this particular instance, also between Falmer and Lewes, it would not be fair to apportion blame in any particular area. Suffice it to say that the engine that blew up was leading a train up the bank at this point, with another engine pushing at the rear. The force of the explosion was reported as sufficient to bend the rails under the engine, while the unfortunate crew were themselves blown off the engine, the driver receiving fatal injuries. The first few wagons were also understandably damaged by the force of the explosion, although Dendy-Marshall quotes that the second vehicle contained two cows that, when taken out, '…began to graze on the embankment, not a bit worse for their adventure'.

The LBSCR's neighbours were of course the two

companies previously mentioned — the South Eastern (later the SECR) and the LSWR — both of which would regularly cast envious eyes at what was recognised as established LBSCR territory. Regarding actual plans for expansion, it was the South Eastern that was probably the greater threat, in that its tentacles reached Guildford and Reading, in so doing threatening to exert a stranglehold on any future plans the LBSCR may itself have had. Competition also existed between the two with regard to shipping services to France, and while it must be said that the route from the Kent coast was by far the most direct, the Newhaven to Dieppe service represented a satisfactory investment for the Brighton concern, and indeed would continue as such under the auspices of the Southern Railway later on.

The political relationships between the LBSCR and its neighbours also show up well in the situation regarding running powers that existed in 1923. At that time the only running powers the LBSCR possessed over the LSWR were from Peasmarsh Junction to Guildford station, while those over the SECR were numerous and involved Bricklayers Arms Junction to Willow Walk Junction, London Bridge to Corbet's Lane Junction, St Leonards to Hastings, Stoats Nest Junction to Redhill via Merstham, Tunbridge Wells (Grove Junction) to Tunbridge Wells SECR or Central station for passenger traffic only, Wandsworth Road Junction to Barrington Road Junction, and Woodside Junction to Woodside Station.

Conflict with the South Western was really confined to Guildford and Portsmouth. At the latter location the matter almost came to blows with the first operation of the Portsmouth 'Direct' line at the end of 1858, after which an uneasy truce existed until the Grouping in 1923. But it was within the London area that conflicts of interest and duplication of routes really existed; such duplications are, however, an advantage nowadays, with the system carrying a far greater volume of passenger traffic than could ever have been envisaged. Even so, there existed what may be described as an acceptance of each neighbour, perhaps the best example being at Clapham Junction, where the LBSCR operated the south side of the station and the LSWR the north. Indeed, in British Railways days almost the same situation would recur, with Central and Western Division services separated, not on the basis of conflict, but purely to keep differing routes separate. The term junction is therefore perhaps slightly inaccurate, for the location is mainly a number of separate routes passing through a single station.

The subject of accidents has been touched on previously, but it may be worth mentioning that today's tendency to invoke litigation at the slightest whim is perhaps not such a new trend after all. Indeed, in June 1869 a collision between a goods train and an excursion would cost the company more than £74,000 in claims, even if some of these were somewhat over-inflated. It is interesting to note that one passenger on the excursion who asked for £3,000 received just £10, while another who requested the same amount was awarded £250!

In 1881 the LBSCR pioneered the use of electric lighting for railway carriages; it was so successful that by 1893 some 300 coaches had been equipped. At the time it was very much a question of where the LBSCR led, others followed. A further example of the forward thinking of the company was in 1898 when it was decreed that all future building of main-line passenger stock would be in the form of bogie vehicles. To achieve this, a new carriage works was established at Lancing, west of Brighton, which would continue to serve the needs of the LBSCR and SR until eventually closed by British Railways. Today the site is an industrial estate, although in the one surviving building from the railway era it is still possible to see former carriage windows etched with their class designations intact in the windows of a modern factory.

In common with Britain's other railway companies, the LBSCR had little in the way of through services penetrating other companies' territories. There were some minor exceptions, but these primarily involved trains reaching a main destination rather than actually penetrating far afield. Indeed, this was the norm for the period; long-distance travel was recognised as involving changes of trains and lines. This altered in 1905 with the introduction of the 'Sunny South Express', which ran between Liverpool and the South Coast, the LBSCR and LNWR changing motive power at Willesden, but with the coaches working through. It could be considered to be another example of the pioneering spirit of the LBSCR — and of course the LNWR — but although successful, it was regarded almost as a novelty.

At the time of the Grouping the LBSCR contributed to the newly formed Southern Railway a route mileage of some 457 miles. Of this, 100 miles was single track and the remainder was at least double track, with 82 miles having three or more lines of rails. In addition there were 355 miles of sidings, while a total of 619 locomotives contributed towards the Southern's engine pool, and it is a credit to the designs as a whole that in percentage terms more LBSCR machines would survive to be taken over by BR in 1948 than those of its neighbours, the SECR and LSWR. This was, as pointed out by R. C. Riley, 'despite the widespread electrification of ex-LBSCR lines'!

As mentioned at the start of this Introduction, the legend of the LBSCR remains as popular today within the railway enthusiast fraternity as that of any other company, regardless of having been one of the smaller English companies. Part of that attraction has to lie in the image of engines painted in Stroudley's yellow livery, while the continuing appeal of the Bluebell Railway has done much to perpetuate this image and ensure that this interest is maintained among later generations. One only has to recall the furore that occurred when British Railways announced that it was to abolish the 'Brighton Belle' service to realise that such nostalgia is not necessarily always confined to the enthusiast. Our railway operators might do well to take notice from the lessons of history.

Kevin Robertson
January 2004

Above:

Understandably, illustrations from the earliest years are restricted to those of contemporary artists and engravers, and it is not until after the mid-19th century that true photographic records become available. One such is this view at Wimbledon station, with Craven well-tank No 14 *Merton* dating from May 1852 at the head of what was then its regular duty from West Croydon. *IAL*

Below:

At Eastbourne in March 1881 Craven 0-4-2T No 369 is coupled to a single six-wheel 1st Class Brake coach. Built at Brighton works in December 1865, this engine first appeared as No 214, but was renumbered as shown in May 1878. It was scrapped in September 1882. *IAL*

12

Early Views

Right:
This LBSCR scene of 1882 was recorded at Uckfield. The locomotive is one of the Dübs-built 2-4-0s of the 242-247 series dating from April 1867, which were renumbered in the 457-462 series in September 1881. The class was withdrawn between 1891 and 1895. *IAL*

Below:
History recalls that the first Bank Holiday legally deemed as such was 7 August 1871. Earlier, Whitsun had been termed a Bank Holiday, but was little observed in fact. This photograph was taken in the early evening of that August Monday and shows Lovers Walk sidings at Brighton with what appears to be a range of assorted Cravens types together with a new Stroudley-design 2-2-2 'Sussex' alongside — 'WS' himself is said to be standing by one of the engines in view. They are all no doubt waiting to back down to Brighton station ready for trains returning to Victoria later in the day. *R. C. Riley collection*

14

Upper left:
One of the earliest views of the LBSCR scene shows Brighton running shed in 1859. Aside from the locomotives, the neat stack of coal and the wagons with both dumb and spring buffers are worthy of note. *Author's collection*

Right:
For piloting trains up the bank at New Cross and also for shunting at Brighton, four 0-6-0T engines were provided. Built at Brighton in 1868, this particular example lasted until October 1893. They were later renumbered in the duplicate list, as seen here. Notice the three-link couplings and wooden buffer beams, while the pannier tanks tend to give a certain Swindon appearance. The engine is seen at Brighton. *IAL*

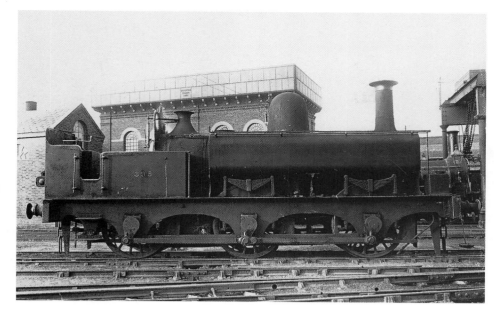

Left:
Built by Slaughter & Co of Bristol in October 1868 and originally numbered 249, this 0-6-0 was later renumbered 468 and is recorded with injectors as well as a Stroudley copper-cap chimney. *IAL*

Below:
Sister engine No 253 is seen in 'as built' condition. The six engines of this type, Nos 249-54, were renumbered 468-73 in the fourth duplicate list in October 1881. Fitted with 5ft-diameter driving wheels and a safety chain in lieu of a conventional front coupling, the engine was recorded at Portsmouth probably shortly after delivery. *IAL*

Lower left:
No 400 was possibly one of the most altered engines ever operated on the LBSCR. Originally built as No 27 in 0-4-0T form, it was later altered to an 0-4-2T type before reverting to the 0-4-0T wheel arrangement. Heavily modified at Brighton works in 1868, it is seen here in 1890 while acting as the Earlswood shunter and displaying Stroudley passenger locomotive livery. *IAL*

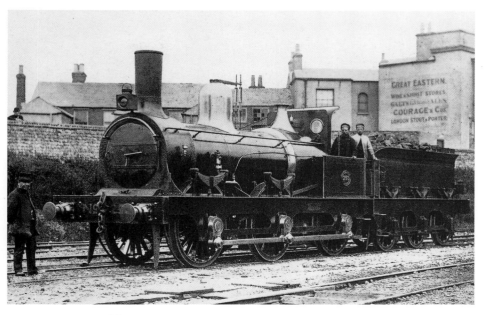

Left:
Old No 4 (later renumbered 104, 295, then 365) is seen awaiting breaking up in 1882. The legend on the side indicates the scrap number (8), the weight and the date of sale, this information being allocated by the foreman at Horley. It is believed that this particular machine was dismantled by the firm of Moss Isaacs. *IAL*

Right:
Built by Robert Stephenson & Co in July 1864, No 195 *Portsmouth* was one of a class of 12 engines that were named in January 1871. Originally stationed at Brighton and used on London services, they were later relegated to lesser duties as the more capable 0-4-2 Stroudley designs began to appear. Renumbered 486 in November 1887, the engine survived until January 1893, although it had enjoyed little work the previous year, with just 13 miles recorded for the whole of 1892.
Author's collection

Left:
This final view of the early period was part of a large volume of sepia prints purchased by the author for a few pounds in 2002; this record of *Dieppe* was the only LBSCR picture in the album, but also one of the finest. This engine was also built by Robert Stephenson & Co in August 1864 and renumbered No 490 in November 1887. Several of the type were rebuilt in various forms, although No 490 remained basically unaltered throughout its existence. The last few months of its life were spent as a pumping engine at Tunbridge Wells, after which it was withdrawn in April 1896.
Author's collection

London Victoria

Above:
The exterior of Victoria station, the LBSCR's principal London terminus, *circa* 1895, when transport was provided by natural horsepower. The scaffolding would clearly indicate building work, which may well also explain the temporary overhead access. *IAL*

Right:
A few decades later, congestion outside Victoria is still a feature, although caused by more modern transport. *IAL*

Left:
This interior view of the LBSCR side of Victoria shows what were classified as the main-line platforms — to Brighton, Lewes, Eastbourne, etc. The view is thought to have been taken *circa* 1910, with a Smith's news-stand in the background. Notice the prominence given to the Gentlemen's facilities, yet aside from the staff most of those visible appear to be female. *IAL*

Upper right:
A relatively quiet Victoria station in 1873. A 'D' class tank can be identified, but otherwise the items of note must be the two milk churns — it is a long time since milk was handled at any of the London termini. *R. C. Riley collection*

Right:
The LBSCR departure board at Victoria. *IAL*

Below:
Victoria was jointly used with the SECR. In LBSCR days, prior to electrification, a Brighton service is seen leaving, while on the far right can just be glimpsed an SECR train. *IAL*

Lower right:
A splendid panorama of Victoria recorded on 18 October 1916, with 'B2X' No 207 in the platform on the right and 'D3' No 369 on the left. *SLS collection*

London Bridge

Left:
London Bridge, south of the Thames, was another joint LBSCR and South Eastern Railway station, seen in c1900, just after the formation of the SECR. Each company maintained separate entrances and platforms, with road power provided, of course, by the horse. Interestingly, in the 19th century, long before the internal combustion engine had been conceived, it was suggested that if equine transport were to continue to increase at the rate it had in recent years, a century later the streets of London could well be four feet deep in manure! Perhaps the motor car did provide some benefit after all. *IAL*

Centre left:
In this 1882 view of London Bridge, at least two 'Terrier' tank locomotives are visible. What is always so apparent in views of main stations and termini at this period is the provision of sidings for storing stock to be attached and detached, as witness what looks to be horse-boxes in the centre road. Later, of course, 'block train' working would negate such a need. *IAL*

Below:
London Bridge *circa* 1925, shortly after the Grouping, and there are already signs of track alterations having taken place. The camera has been positioned to give a good view of the lines of what were once the two separate companies' lines, the LBSCR to the left and SECR on the right. Notice that even in what are now Southern Railway days, the two concerns appeared to maintain their own stock working over their own lines. The small locomotive depot is well and truly sandwiched! *IAL*

Above:
A guard's-eye view from the 5.40pm London Bridge to East Grinstead approaching East Croydon in 1951 with Atlantic No 32421 *South Foreland* in charge. The train is just about to pass under what was then the largest surviving gantry of former LBSCR signals. *P. J. Lynch*

Brighton Main Line

Right:
Judging from the LNWR stock, this may well be the 'Sunny South Express' which ran between Liverpool and the South Coast. 'B4' No 61 is in charge during the climb towards Quarry Tunnel.
E. T. Vyse/J. H. Price

Left:
The exterior of the station buildings at Horley. The track here was later quadrupled, and it is believed that the building depicted dates from when the platform loops were added. The lack of any vehicular traffic is apparent. *IAL*

Centre left:
The station at Balcombe, south of Three Bridges, is just visible under the bridge. The tall co-acting signal arms were a boon to drivers approaching from any distance, although the job of the lampman, or lad, was perhaps not to be envied.
R. C. Riley collection

Right:
This is Wivelsfield Junction according to the card, but it was officially known as Keymer Junction, north of Burgess Hill. Looking south, the main Brighton line continues straight ahead and that to Lewes diverges to the left. The signalbox here had been in existence since at least 1886 — the 'box on stilts' type was a design favoured by the LBSCR, affording good visibility over a wide area. Incidentally, the last signalbox of this type operating on former LBSCR lines was at Hardham Junction, and remained operational well into BR days. *IAL*

Wivelsfield Junction. Burgess Hill, Sussex.

Above:
A Stroudley tender engine approaches Burgess Hill station from the north. The men proudly posing for the camera could well be company staff, possibly from the Civil Engineer's department. *IAL*

Centre left:
On the outskirts of Brighton is Preston Park, seen here with an unidentified member of the 'B4' class. *IAL*

Right:
Preston Viaduct at Brighton carried the coast line east towards Lewes. This photograph is purported to have been taken in 1858, when the area was devoid of the urban sprawl that would later take place, while the South Downs are likewise untouched, the railway itself an intrusion in the landscape. *R. C. Riley collection*

Brighton Station

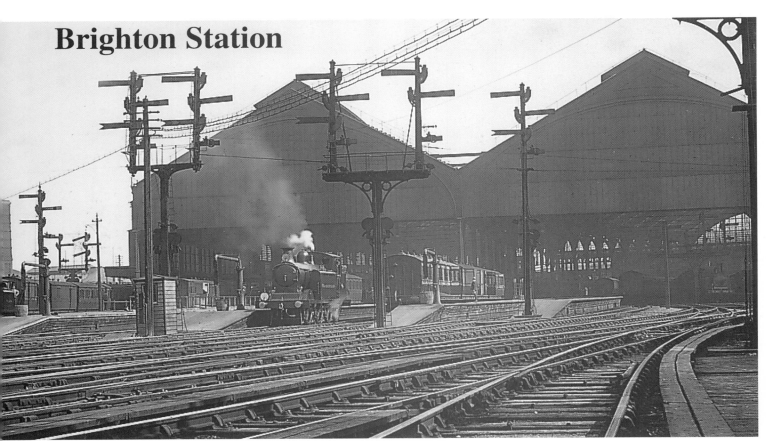

Upper left:
The terminus at Brighton was, in LBSCR days, known as Brighton Central. Visible in the centre is 'E5' tank No 402 *Wanborough*, while on the left is 'D1' No 294, then named *Rosebery*. *IAL*

Lower left:
The curving platforms of Brighton are seen on a card posted on 3 January 1907 (the addressee was in South Africa and the card carried a 1d stamp!). The picture contains a wealth of detail: the horse-drawn cabs, luggage-van, advertising posters and the number of short six-wheel vehicles still in service. The main train is hauled by a 'B4' 4-4-0 and comprise of bogie stock. *IAL*

Above right:
The Edwardian era at Brighton: horse-drawn cabs in the station forecourt. *IAL*

Right:
One of the approaches to Brighton station — not the main entrance, of course, but seen instead from what is now a very busy Terminus Road, looking east. The Trafalgar Street bridge under the station forecourt still survives, although the canopy has been altered; the buffer stops of the terminus are located to the left and out of view. *IAL*

25

London Suburbs

Above:
A May 1957 view of part of Clapham Junction, showing the former LBSCR route crossing the West London line. A former LBSCR 'C2X', No 32553, is at the head of a train of track panels. *H. C. Casserley*

Below:
South of Clapham Junction is Wandsworth Common station. Electrification has taken place, but a steam-hauled Victoria–Battersea–West Croydon–Sutton (via Balham line) service is passing through hauled by an 'E5' 0-6-2T. *IAL*

Right:
Thornton Heath station is located between Streatham and Selhurst. This was one of many stations within the London suburban area where traffic developed far in excess of what could ever have been anticipated, leading to subsequent electrification. *IAL*

Centre right:
This is the LBSCR at Selhurst, also prior to electrification. South of the station were three junctions, the main line heading towards East Croydon while to the left a route turned north to Norwood and another to the right southwest towards West Croydon. *IAL*

Below:
A wonderful portrait of 'E3' No 459 passing Honor Oak Park, on the main line from London Bridge towards Norwood (not to be confused with the nearby SECR station at Honor Oak). The 'E3s' were at first employed on suburban passenger duties; in 1894/5 No 459 was one of seven based in the London area. *IAL*

Above:
The exterior of Sutton station provides a somewhat bland appearance, although it is perhaps partly relieved by the ornate brickwork below each gable. *IAL*

Below:
This is Cheam station, as rebuilt, with 0-6-0T No 230 arriving at the head of a lengthy train of four- and six-wheel stock. Such services were of course ripe for electrification in later years, as indeed would be the case here. *IAL*

Above:
We are now in rural Sussex, and this is the view from the footplate of a 'C2X' approaching West Dean Tunnel between Lavant and Singleton on the Chichester to Midhurst route. *IAL*

Rural Lines and Branches

Right:
Rudgwick was on the line between Guildford and Christ's Hospital, and was perhaps typical of the country station of the Victorian period in that it provided a useful service to the community — witness the packed yard, with wagons containing a variety of goods, and of course the passenger train in the platform. *IAL*

Above:
Betchworth Tunnel lay on the LBSCR south of Dorking, not to be confused with the station of the same name on the nearby SECR line. 'D3' No 363 *Goldsmid* is in charge of an up service. Renamed *Havant* in September 1895, this was the last of the class to lose both its name and its Stroudley yellow livery, in March 1913. It was also the first of the type to be built in June 1892 and had achieved 1.4 million miles before being withdrawn on the eve of nationalisation in December 1947. *IAL*

Below:
Serving the Sussex Downs high above Brighton, the branch to The Dyke, 3 miles 49 chains long, diverged from the main coastal line between Hove and Portslade and was single track with a run-round loop at the terminus. The gradients show up well here as 'I3' No 2033 runs round its train. It was the practice for engines working the branch always to face uphill; in that way there was a guarantee of the firebox crown remaining covered with water. *R. C. Riley collection*

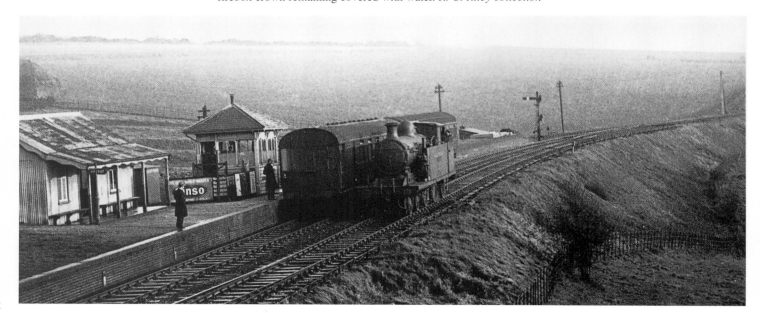

Right:
A 1938 scene at The Dyke, with the permanent way department engaged on track maintenance. This was not long before closure of the branch, which took place on 1 January 1939.
R. C. Riley collection

Centre right:
The majority of custom for The Dyke branch was seasonal and comprised day-trippers, walkers and hikers. Even so there was also some freight, mainly agricultural from the farms dotted high on the downs. Here a 'D1' class tank waits to return with its train to Brighton, while the wagons will also no doubt be collected and returned shortly. *R. C. Riley collection*

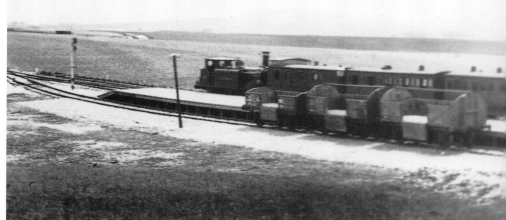

Below:
Another branch from Brighton led to Kemp Town, very much the poor relation. Opened in 1869, this branch off the main line, just 1 mile 32 chains long, involved considerable civil engineering in the form of a 14-arch viaduct and a tunnel 946yd long. Due to its tortuous route it was an early casualty to street competition, and passenger services ceased in 1933. There was one intermediate station at Lewes Road, which after closure to passengers was for many years a pickle factory.
R. C. Riley

Above:
This is Cowden on the Oxted – Edenbridge–Groombridge line, looking north towards Hever. Opened in 1881, this 12½-mile route was built by a nominally independent concern largely along the course of the abandoned works of the former Surrey & Sussex Junction Railway. It was operated by the LBSCR from the outset. *R. C. Riley collection*

Centre left:
West of Groombridge station was a triangle formed by the lines to Cowden, Eridge and Tunbridge Wells. Adding some confusion was the fact that in LBSCR days the eastern and southern points of the triangle were both simply referred to as Groombridge Junction. At the northwest end of the triangle stood Ashurst Junction, which was in addition the divergence of the single line west through Forest Row to East Grinstead. The Groombridge signalbox stands at the forefront of this photograph. *IAL*

Lower left:
The LBSCR designations and identity have of course long vanished from Hailsham station on the Groombridge–Polegate line in this early 1960s photograph, although green enamel signs from the Southern era remain prominent. The author is perhaps ashamed to admit that he recalls the collection of motor vehicle marques only too well — Morris Minor, Ford Anglia, Ford Prefect and Wolseley… *IAL*

Along the Coast

Portsmouth & Southsea was a joint LBSCR/LSWR terminus at the extreme western end of the former's coastal lines. This aerial view was taken in 1931 in Southern Railway days, with the passenger facilities to the left and the then extensive goods department on the right. *IAL*

Chichester station was extensively rebuilt soon after the Grouping and here plays host to 'I3' No 2029 on a coastal working in 1924, with the rebuilding in evidence. No 2029 is waiting to depart westwards for Portsmouth, where the engine will probably come off ready to work back east to Brighton. *S. Oborne*

Upper left:
Drayton station, east of Chichester, opened on 8 June 1846, but was closed by the Southern from 1 June 1930, although the line itself remained opened. Today little if anything remains to indicate that a stopping place ever existed, unlike further along the coast at Yapton, where the station of that name was also an early casualty, yet one platform and the main building still survive. *IAL*

Above:
Ford railway bridge spanned the River Arun just east of Ford station, and is shown here in the open position ready for the passage of vessels, at a time when shipping would still venture inland to Arundel and beyond. The coast line here was later electrified, in July 1938. *IAL*

Lower left:
A delightful view of Barnham Junction taken around the end of the 19th century — notice the slotted-post signals, and the divergence of the Bognor branch line on the right. The signalbox represents one of the standard types of architecture for medium to large boxes on the system; few of this type survive today, although fortunately one still stands not far away at Chichester, its future now certain as a listed structure. *R. C. Riley collection*

Above:
In this view, Shoreham, on the main coast line between Brighton and Worthing, is seen, looking west *circa* 1886. The signalbox was located so as to afford a good view of the road level crossing nearby, which today is the scene of considerable congestion every time the barriers are operated. *IAL*

Above:
This is the south end of Lewes with the photographer facing Wivelsfield, with a 'B4' 4-4-0 destined for Newhaven, Eastbourne or Hastings. *SLS collection*

Upper right:
On the approach to the terminus at
Eastbourne, the engine is identified as a
Stroudley double-framed 'B' type. The
railway reached the coastal town in 1849
with the completion of the branch from
Polegate, although at the time the original
station was described as little more than a
hut. A second station was erected in 1866,
although the well-known 'Brighton
baroque' façade that survives today was not
added until 1886. Further rebuilding with a
more spacious concourse and longer
platforms in connection with electrification
occurred under the Southern Railway in
1935. *IAL*

Lower right:
A Brighton to Ashford service via Hastings
is seen at Rye on former SECR metals, but
with one of the LBSCR's celebrated
'Gladstones', No 174 — once named
Fratton — at its head. The engine is
carrying Southern livery, clearly dating the
view after 1923, and the train is indicative
of the type of relatively light duties then
entrusted to the class, which dated back as
far as 1882. The cascading of more engines
to these duties would foretell the end of the
class, and No 174 was withdrawn in 1929,
by which time only a very few of remained
in active service, the last being withdrawn
in 1932. *R. C. Riley collection*

Above:
The east end of Lewes, with the Eastbourne and Newhaven line curving to the right and
that to Uckfield and Tunbridge Wells on the left. Also on the left is a line of cattle wagons
and horse-boxes. It will be noted that even the timber of the board crossing is neatly laid
and in good and clean condition. *R. C. Riley collection*

Below:
Much later, in BR days in 1950, 'I3' tank No 32076 heads a Birmingham to Hastings
restaurant car express across Southerham lift bridge. *S. C. Nash*

Views from the Tilling Collection

Before taking a look at the various locomotive works on the LBSCR system, it would be appropriate to include a selection of photographs taken of the LBSCR by W. G. Tilling, whose book *Locomotives of the Brighton & South Coast Railway* was published in 1923, and kindly made available by Brian Arman, who has been an invaluable source of illustrations. Most were taken at Brighton shed and works, but the first provides a further view of Lewes.

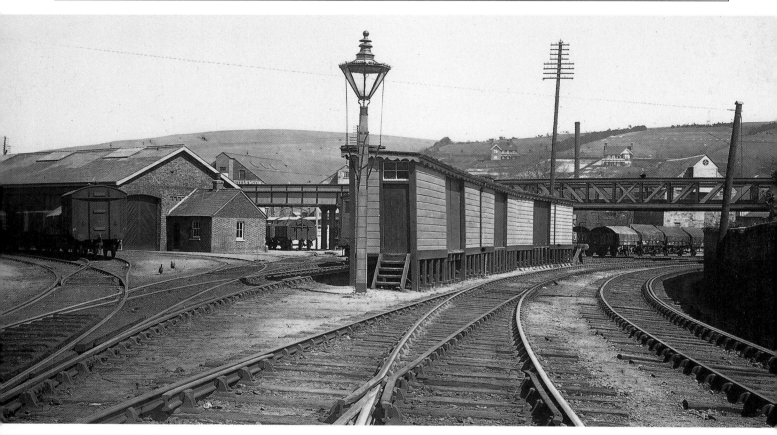

Above:
A wonderful track-level view of the goods facilities at Lewes, with a variety of tarpaulin-covered wagons in the distance. Notice the solitary gas lamp, no doubt sufficient for most work in the days before widespread 'light pollution'. *W. G. Tilling*

Left:
'B4' class 4-4-0 No 45 *Duchess of Fife* receiving attention at Brighton running shed. The use of the breakdown crane — a 15 ton Cowan & Sheldon machine — to assist in dropping the bogie is interesting. Does this mean the running shed did not have a set of shear-legs? *W. G. Tilling*

Right:

'B4' No 45, later named *Bessborough*, is under construction at Brighton, 1902. It was the only member of the class to be fitted with Drummond firebox cross-tubes. Although in theory an excellent idea in increasing the heating area, in practice poor water circulation caused internal corrosion and pitting, so any advantage gained was minimal, and the cross-tubes were later removed. It would be left to Oliver Bulleid, decades later, to succeed in a similar method with his use of thermic siphons.
W. G. Tilling

Below:

Another 'B4', No 54 *Empress*, is seen within the works. The overhead crane — presumably electrically operated — appears capable of not only lifting but also slewing, and as such would allow for maximum occupancy of available space. *W. G. Tilling*

Upper left:
New boilers delivered to Brighton works. While the works did both construct and repair boilers, outside contractors were also used, this particular batch bearing the reference '1378' and apparently consisting of at least four of like type. *W. G. Tilling*

Lower left:
Inside Brighton's boiler shop are a number of what look to be 'B4'-type boilers. The third from the camera — inverted — would appear to have not yet had its inner firebox fitted, which could well explain the reason for the gantry positioned directly overhead. *W. G. Tilling*

Above right:
In the same shop, this boiler barrel is waiting to have a new firebox fitted. *W. G. Tilling*

Above:
This time the boiler is from an 'E1' tank — identified by the Ramsbottom-type safety valve and the large closed dome. Of particular interest, however, are the works tramway systems, one involving a turntable and the narrower-gauge one taking a deliberate swerve around its circumference. On the left the indicator is pointing to a pressure of some 80psi — possibly compressed air for the boiler-making tools — while to the right the notice warns that 'Smoking is strictly prohibited in these works'. *W. G. Tilling*

Upper right:
Open storage of spare material, in particular tyres and timber, at the rear of the works. *W. G. Tilling*

Upper right:
Open storage of spare material, in particular tyres and timber, at the rear of the works. *W. G. Tilling*

Lower right:
Extension of the accommodation, which took place at a number of dates, including major works in 1873, 1878 and 1881. *W. G. Tilling*

Above:
An assortment of Marsh boilers, some of which have apparently been assembled outside the works simply due to restrictions on space within. Clearly the wagon brakes are not working, hence the presence of the sprag in the spokes. Could they be new boilers for rebuilding Class C2 engines to 'C2X' form? *W. G. Tilling*

Below:
An exterior view of part of the office complex at Brighton, including the drawing office. The view may well have been taken during one of the periods of expansion, as witness the part-demolished wall at the far end. *W. G. Tilling*

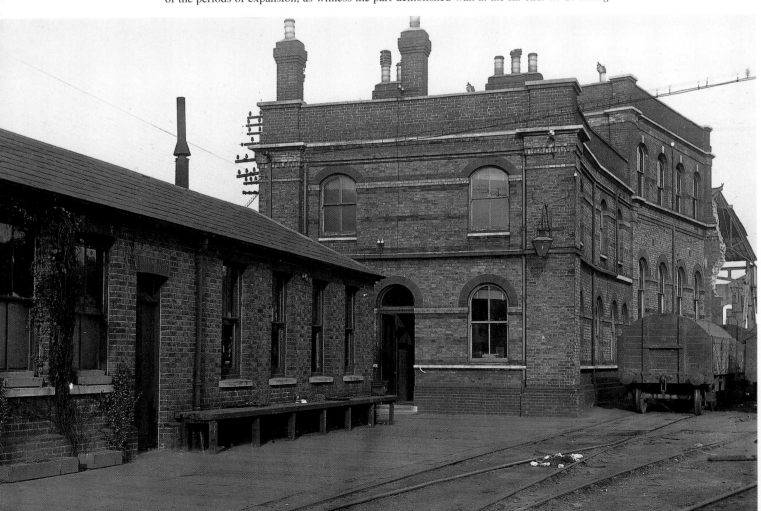

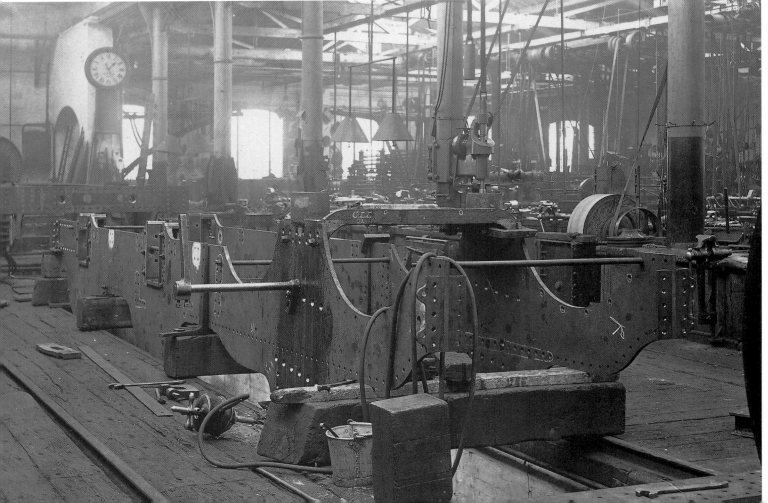

Upper left:
The interior of the machine shop, with its belt drives, so typical of engineering workshops of the period, shown to advantage. *W. G. Tilling*

Lower left:
It is 1.25pm, and the inverted frames of a 'B4' are under construction at Brighton. Only the first three and the last five 'B4s' — of a class total of 33 — were actually built or assembled at the South Coast works, as existing repair commitments meant that the majority were sourced from Messrs Sharp, Stewart & Co in Glasgow, hence their nickname 'Scotchmen'. Despite being generally successful engines, this view is interesting in depicting what was to become the Achilles' heel of the class, a weakness in the frames over the driving axles; indeed, in later years the frames would be considerably patched or plated above the horns. *W. G. Tilling*

Above:
At least three types of locomotive are identifiable within the erecting shop. On the right is an 'E' tank, while it is also just possible to make out a 'B2' and a 'B4'. *W. G. Tilling*

Above:
Another erecting shop view shows a variety of Marsh and Stroudley types in various states of undress. The presence of a single-wheeler — in the right-hand group towards the rear — is interesting: was it being cannibalised for spares? *W. G. Tilling*

Above:
Former LBSCR 'Terrier' tank *Fenchurch* is seen unnumbered and in lined black, possibly therefore recorded around 1898, at which time it had been sold to the Newhaven Harbour Company for the sum of £350. Notice the wooden brake blocks. This engine returned to the Southern in February 1927 consequent upon the takeover of the harbour undertaking and was then allocated the number 636. Eventually becoming BR No 32636, it achieved an estimated total mileage in excess of 1.1 million in a 93-year lifespan, which has no doubt been added to as it was subsequently preserved on the Bluebell Railway. *W. G. Tilling*

Left:
These completed locomotives were probably photographed around 1905 (based on an assumption that the nearest locomotive, No 411, is an 'E6' built in that year and appears to be in works primer, possibly therefore awaiting its first painting). Also identifiable are a 'B4', two 'C2s', another 4-4-0, then a Stroudley machine — the rest cannot be positively discerned. Notice in particular the hanging gas pipes that branch out laterally to form what would have been a crude but effective means of illumination. *W. G. Tilling*

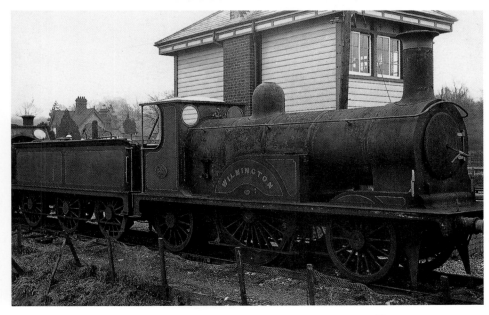

Above and left:
As intimated earlier, capacity at Brighton works was severely restricted around the turn of the 19th century due to a backlog of repairs, and the amount of spare capacity for new work was therefore limited. A consequence of this was also the limited space available for storage of locomotives awaiting either repair or scrap, and at least three large concentrations of engines awaiting works decisions were established at East Grinstead, Horley and Horsted Keynes. Among those identified at here at Horsted Keynes are singles *Southbourne* and *Wilmington*, while the boy is standing next to another unidentified member of the class. Few would be repaired to run again. *W. G. Tilling*

Lower left:
Concluding the selection from Brian Arman's collection of W. G. Tilling photographs is this close-up view of the opposite side of No 343 *Wilmington*, posed at the rear of Horsted Keynes signalbox and close to the junction of the line to Ardingly. Ironically, after withdrawal several of the class found their way to Italy or Japan, where their scrap value was greater, despite the cost of sea transit. No 343 was actually withdrawn in June 1907, although together with several others of the type it had achieved little actual running mileage for some months before this. Note that the Westinghouse brake has already been removed. *W. G. Tilling*

Railway Works

Above:

As mentioned in the previous section, at least three large concentrations of engines awaiting works decisions were established at East Grinstead, Horley and Horsted Keynes. The line-up includes 'E' class tank No 146 *Havre*, 'E4' No 516 *Rustington*, 'B4' No 51 and 'E4' No 476 *Beeding*, followed by another of the same class, No 478 *Newick*, after which come a 'C1' 0-6-0, another 'E4' and two 'B4' 4-4-0s. The view was taken on the new Ashurst Spur, which, at that time (c1906/7), had not yet opened for traffic. *IAL*

Right:
This is the paint shop at what is believed to be Brighton works (there is some discussion that due to restricted space locomotives were taken to the nearby carriage works at Lancing for final painting, and while this may have been done on certain occasions it is not believed to have been the regular practice). Three 'B4' 4-4-0s are visible, the nearest being No 54 *Empress*, which only carried that name from new in May 1900 until August 1906, when it was renamed *Princess Royal*. Up to this time LBSCR engines had never carried cast nameplates, the names instead being painted on the splashers or tank sides, although this would change later. To the rear are some Billinton-designed tanks, either of the 'E4' or 'E5' type. Again the provision of the gas lighting equipment will be noted.
R. C. Riley collection

Right:
It is 1911 at Brighton works, and construction of the Atlantics in the series 421-6 is under way. Together with the earlier series, numbered 37-41, which had been built by Kitson & Co, they were later named by the Southern after coastal locations served by the railway. They were also destined to be the largest passenger tender engines built by the LBSCR, with a number providing sterling service to its successor, the Southern, and on into BR days. *IAL*

Below:
The first of the pair of 'J' class tanks — this one would become No 325 *Abergavenny* — under construction at Brighton works in December 1910. Intended for the fast services between Brighton and Victoria, the two engines, while outwardly similar, had a number of minor variations, but both were regarded as strong, reliable performers and were popular with their crews. The man in centre of the group standing is John Pelham-Maitland, LBSCR enthusiast and later shed foreman at Newhaven and Nine Elms. *IAL*

Left:
Stripped for repair, this is No 325 in Brighton works. The asbestos lagging is conspicuous, and was widely used in railway workshops at the time.
R. C. Riley collection

Centre left:
'D1' 0-4-2T No 267 *Maresfield* is partly stripped, possibly pending overhaul. Built by Neilson & Co under works number 2736 in May 1882, examples of this numerous class were to be found throughout the LBSCR system, and later also migrated over former SECR and LSWR lines. Withdrawals commenced early on, and with the spread of electrification a number of the class had little work. No 267 was one of the casualties, being taken out of service in January 1935. *IAL*

Right:
In Southern days as No 2325, and displaying 'Bulleid' livery, the shell of what had formerly been *Abergavenny* awaits being reunited with its boiler at Eastleigh works on 31 May 1947. There being only two members in the class, no spare boiler was ever provided, although over the years a number of new fireboxes were fitted. Accordingly, if the boiler required repair it could result in long periods out of service — as here — although both engines would survive to be renumbered by British Railways and were active until 1951. *IAL*

Right:
The first of what would be designated the 'H2' class of Atlantics is in works grey at Brighton and reportedly brand-new, presumably therefore photographed in 1911. The reason for its lifting is unclear — was there a defect on what was a new engine? According to Bradley, the class displayed a trait of stopping at 'top dead centre', under which circumstance they would neither move forward nor back. The same criticism would be levelled years later at Bulleid with his sleeve valve experiment on what would be 'H1' No 2039. Perhaps, then, it was not the sleeve valves after all! It is doubtful also that the headcode as displayed by the position of the lamps applies for the present — Victoria to Hastings, and London Bridge and Wimbledon! *IAL*

Above:
'I3' No 25 is being attended to on the wheel drop at Brighton running shed in 1920. The engine is for the present bereft of both pairs of driving wheels, that with the crank axle being a useful leaning point for the artisan nearby. Superheated from new, No 25 has already had a replacement chimney fitted, and survived into BR days as No 32025 until withdrawal in January 1950. *A. B. Macleod*

Tender Locomotives

'G' Class Singles

Above:

No 325 *Abergavenny* was the first of the Stroudley 'G' class of small singles, which ran to 26 engines. All were named, although as in this case many had no relevance to locations served by the LBSCR! Numbered 325-350, they emerged from Brighton from January 1877 onwards and, as would be expected, survived a number of modifications over their lifetime, although the changes — continuous handrails, cast-iron driving wheels — do not appear have been consistently applied to all members of the class. Despite having the limited adhesion of a single-wheel type, the class was gainfully employed on a variety of routes, including the Tunbridge Wells, Eastbourne and Portsmouth services, well into the first decade of the 20th century. *Abergavenny* lasted until June 1909, and was reportedly withdrawn when it failed to keep time on a train from Lewes on which Marsh was a passenger. This was despite the fact that there was evidently nothing wrong with the engine and that the poor time-keeping had been solely due to excessive slipping caused by extremely wet weather. *Author's collection*

Left:
An interesting view of a tenderless No 325 — with a workman posing for the camera. One of the first engines to work services along the new direct line from Tunbridge Wells via Edenbridge to London in late 1887, it was soon displaced by engines having more than just a single pair of driving wheels. Just nine years later it was again heavily criticised when a train it was hauling arrived late in London, leading to a director of the LBSCR missing his onward connection at King's Cross! *SLS collection*

Above:
'G' class No 326 *Grosvenor* is seen at Battersea probably towards the turn of the 20th century. Built at Brighton at the end of 1874 for a recorded cost of £3,074 — excluding tender — the engine originally carried the number 151, but this was changed to that seen in December 1880. The clasp brakes were added around 1900 together with the Westinghouse pump, after which the engine had about seven years of working life, being withdrawn in May 1907. The type was extinct by 1914. *SLS collection*

Below:
Close examination reveals someone apparently taking a brief respite on the footplate of No 328 *Sutherland* at what is likely to be Littlehampton. The date is probably some time during the period 1902-8. *SLS collection*

Left:
No 330 *Newhaven* is seen not far from its namesake location — the view is believed to have been taken at Lewes. Only one member of the crew is visible — it is likely that the driver is oiling around — and the view was clearly taken in the winter, as witness the bare branches and numerous nests among the tree-tops. *SLS collection*

Centre left:
Many 'G' class single-wheelers were named after South of England locations — this is No 332 *Shanklin* in a view dated 30 August 1902, by which time it was already 21 years old. Revered by the older drivers and treated with equal disdain by younger men, the singles did sterling work on the Victoria–Portsmouth trains. This particular machine lasted until March 1910. *SLS collection*

Lower left:
A stunning portrait of 'G' class 2-2-2 No 334 *Petworth* at Croydon, in Stroudleys improved engine green'. The posed crew add much to the view, in a location that a century later sees no shunting of trains and little aside from the swish electric efficiency of the modern network. *SLS collection*

'B1' 0-4-2 'Gladstones'

Right:
The 'Richmond' class of 0-4-2s was the smaller predecessor to the 'Gladstones'. This is No 212 *Hartington* at St Leonards West Marina. Just six of the type were built, No 212 appearing in 1880. It had a working life of some 23 years, its number changing to 512 in 1897 and finally 612 in 1900/1. *IAL*

Above:
Namesake of the class itself, No 214 *Gladstone* of 1882 was the first of the type. This was the final design of express engine produced during the tenure of William Stroudley. The engine has yet to be fitted with injectors — for the present just a feed pump is provided — while if the combination of lights is to be believed, the engine is on a London Bridge to Portsmouth working — although photographed on the Brighton turntable! *SLS collection*

Above:
Withdrawn in 1927, *Gladstone* had by then lost its name and had been renumbered by the SR as No 172. Fortunately, upon withdrawal the Southern was receptive to an approach for its preservation, and after restoration it was placed on display at York. In the background is the distinctive outline of an 'Schools' 4-4-0 cab. *IAL*

Below:
No 181 — formerly named *Croydon* — was built at Brighton in 1890. The engine has by now been reboilered, and the crew are no doubt hoping that no locomotive inspectors are around, judging by the amount of smoke! *IAL*

Right:
Cab detail of 'B1' 'Gladstone' No 198, after having been fitted with a new boiler by Marsh in 1906. Clearly the driver was expected to perform his duties while standing, although interestingly there is a seat of sorts available for the fireman. *IAL*

Below:
'Gladstone' No 200 — formerly *Beresford* — is seen in the post-1905 Marsh livery, by which time it had also been fitted with an injector. The tender full of coal is itself worthy of a second glance and has no doubt contributed to the excess of steam from the safety valves! *SLS collection*

'C' Class 0-6-0s

Above:
Although better known as a passenger railway, the LBSCR did have its share of freight. However, the type of traffic involved could not compare with that originating from the industrialised areas of South Wales, the Midlands or the North, and consequently the locomotive types used for goods could not be designed for one type of traffic alone. This is Stroudley-designed 'C1' 0-6-0 No 427, which entered service in May 1884 as part of the second batch of the type, on which the reversing rod was placed outside the firebox lagging instead of running through it, as on earlier engines. The tender has a wonderful load of good-quality coal on board; this may well be needed as engines of the class were regularly employed on the Battersea–Lillie Bridge–Brighton coal trains, which were sometimes made up to 45-50 loaded four-wheel vehicles. The location is Battersea, popular with contemporary photographers; indeed, with the limited film speeds of the time, photographs of stationary engines and trains were far more commonplace. No 427 survived in traffic until March 1911.
SLS collection

Upper right:
Another view of No 427. Behind the engine is brake-van No 151, a Stroudley-built vehicle from the 1870/80s, fitted with the customary wooden brake blocks of the period. The location is believed to be Lewes. *IAL*

Lower right:
An unidentified 'C2' 0-6-0 is working hard on the approach to Groombridge from the direction of Tunbridge Wells. The crew are evidently well aware of the presence of the photographer — was the smoke effect to order? *IAL*

Above:
A line of tarpaulin-covered open wagons — which may very well contain straw, hence the covers — are headed by the first of the 'C2X' rebuilds, No 545, at Willow Walk in July 1908. All but 10 of the 'C2' class were rebuilt in this fashion; the non-rebuilt engines were the earliest casualties of the class, the majority having gone prior to nationalisation. *IAL*

Below:
The 'C2Xs' continued to provide useful service to the Southern Region until the late 1950s, the last to go being No 523 in February 1962. Here, two survivors meet at Wallington, both retaining their original tenders. Others of the type were later fitted with Drummond LSWR tender bodies mounted on the LBSCR frames. *D. Sellman*

'B' Class 4-4-0s

Above:
The R. J. Billinton-designed 'B2' 4-4-0s were referred to by crews as 'Grasshoppers' due to the quality of the ride experienced, although this criticism seemed to fade in later years. Here, No 315 *Duncannon* is thought to be on a Brighton to East Grinstead via Horsted Keynes working. Originally built in July 1895, the engine was converted to 'B2X' form in March 1909 and was finally withdrawn in April 1930, having achieved a total of slightly more than 1.3 million miles. *IAL*

Below:
'B2' No 205 *Hackworth* — several were named after the early pioneers of the Industrial Revolution — is seen in basically original condition. The class had a propensity to create a 'fug', at a time when the emission of smoke was a disciplinary offence, and several crews fell foul of this regulation. In later years No 205 was fitted with a vacuum ejector for working coaches fitted with that type of brake. Withdrawal came as a result of the ever-spreading tentacles of electrification in the early 1930s. *IAL*

Upper left:
'B2' No 320 *Rastrick* stands at Chichester on an evening Victoria–Sutton–Portsmouth excursion in the summer of 1901. Fitted with 6ft 9in driving wheels, this engine had been built at Brighton in 1896, and in 1905 was experimentally painted dark green. Unfortunately, what was a very attractive livery lined out in gold leaf did not find favour with the company directors. The engine was later rebuilt as a 'B2X' in 1910, and as such lasted until 1930. *IAL*

Lower left:
On what could very well be a special working, 'B2' No 171 *Nevill* was photographed in 1898 at rest in Brighton station after arrival, with the 12-wheel Royal Saloon next to the locomotive. The engine at this time was no more than 18 months old. *W. J. Reynolds*

Above:
A 'B2' is double-heading with a Stroudley 'G' at an unknown location, although it could well be Balham or Tooting Bec. Possibly an empty stock working in view of the mix of coaching stock. *IAL*

Below:
At the head of a train of Pullman coaches — including as the lead vehicle what was known as a 'Pullman Pup', used as a generator vehicle to provide the necessary electrical power for the train — this unidentified 'B2' is believed to be somewhere between Croydon and Three Bridges. *IAL*

Above:
'B2X' 4-4-0 No 317 is seen around March 1913, by which time it had lost its original name of *Gerald Loder*. Originally built in June 1896 as a 'B2', the names had been removed from most of the class by 1905. The indicator shelter was in connection with trials then being carried out following the fitting of a feed water heater and Weir pump — both were subsequently removed. The engine is in the Marsh livery with the full 'LB&SCR' on the tender. It was withdrawn in June 1929. *SLS collection*

Upper left:
No 321, formerly *John Rennie*, is seen as newly rebuilt to 'B2X' form in October 1907. As such it survived until September 1930 and achieved something in the order of 1.2 million miles in service. *IAL*

Lower left:
'B2X' No B171 is on an unidentified working at an unidentified location — though probably somewhere on the former LSWR system. The coaching stock is certainly LSWR in origin, while to the left may well be a Adams 'T1' tank. *IAL*

Right:
A wonderful panoramic view of the unique 'B3' No 213 *Bessemer* at speed; unfortunately, further information as to the working and location is not given. *IAL*

Left:
'B4' 4-4-0 No 45 *Bessborough* is seen when it was fitted with the firebox cross-tubes referred to earlier; it is also in yellow livery. Notice the three-link front coupling, which appears to have been typical on tender locomotives. The covers protecting the firebox tubes led to an amusing and fortunately not fatal accident to the driver of the engine late at night on 17 October 1906. Apparently the engine was hauling empty stock at no more than 20mph, so the driver decided to leave the cab and walk around the footplate to administer oil as necessary — this was a common practice at the time. However, on returning to the cab he evidently forgot about the bulbous extensions, bumped into them and fell off on to the track. Fortunately the accident was witnessed by the fireman, who quickly stopped the train and recovered his driver. *SLS collection*

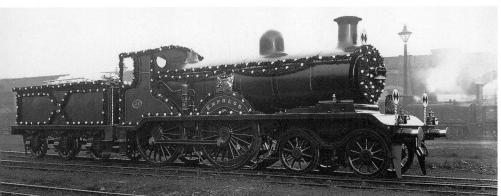

Centre left:
'B4' No 54 *Empress* is seen at Battersea some time between its building in May 1900 and August 1906, after which date it was renamed *Princess Royal*. The decoration is for a Station Masters' special working, although further details of this are not recorded. *IAL*

Right:
Delivery of a Scottish-built 'B4' — notice the lack of coupling rods — behind a 'C2' 0-6-0. Since the various members of the Sharp, Stewart & Co-built 'B4s' were delivered between June and October 1901, it is reasonable to assume that the photograph was taken at this period. Delivery of the engines was from the North through New Cross, so the location must be somewhere between New Cross and Brighton. *IAL*

Above:

An interesting collection of stock behind 'B4' No 61 *Ladysmith*. The engine has been modified with a Marsh short-smokebox boiler and a Marsh chimney. It is also vacuum-fitted for working the 'Sunny South Express' service. *R. C. Riley collection*

Below:

No 61 again, this time at the head of the 'Sunny South Express' passing Purley North. This working was from the LNWR to Eastbourne, hence the need for the vacuum-fitted locomotive. The engine is still in Marsh livery and retains its brass numberplate on the cabside; these were later removed in favour of simple painted numerals. *IAL*

Above:
The 'B4' seen here at Eastbourne is No 69 *Bagshot*. This interesting view also shows steam railmotor No 1. The LBSCR possessed just two railmotors of this type, although it was also involved in the joint cars operated with the LSWR on the East Southsea branch. Of only limited success, the vehicles were incapable of hauling additional vehicles at peak times, so the design was never perpetuated. Both steam vehicles were laid aside during World War 1, although official withdrawal did not take place until 1919. *IAL*

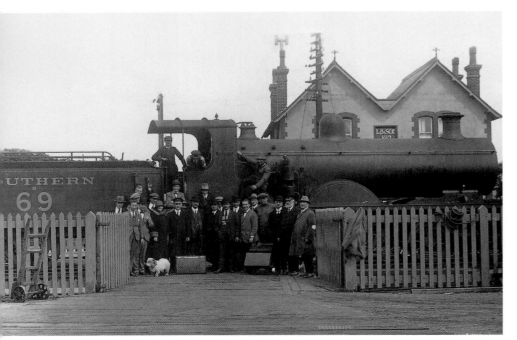

Left:
At what is believed to be Newhaven, this enthusiasts' outing was organised by J. Pelham-Maitland some time prior to 1933, at the time when he was the Newhaven Shed Master. A number of organised visits were arranged in this way, including trips to France. The locomotive is 'B4' No B69 with a Marsh boiler and extended smokebox. *R. C. Riley collection*

Above:
In Southern Railway days, near Southerham Junction, Lewes, a down special Newhaven boat train is captured immediately after leaving the Eastbourne line in August 1937. 'B4X' No 2056 has but five miles further to travel before reaching its destination. *C. C. B. Herbert*

Above:
Prince of Wales was a 'B4' that remained basically unaltered throughout its life from 1902 to 1936. However, the engines that remained in original condition were the first to be withdrawn, while those rebuilt to 'B4X' form all survived into BR days. The photograph was taken at Brighton. *IAL*

'H' Class 4-4-2 Atlantics

Left:
A wonderful head-on view of Marsh 'H1' class 4-4-2 Atlantic No 40, named *St Catherine's Point* by the Southern Railway, in as-built original condition. The combination of lights and discs is a mystery, while the spotless condition is a credit to the cleaners, yet was by no means uncommon at the time. *IAL*

Below:
The train of Pullman cars behind No 39 *La France* clearly indicates the type of prestige working with which the Atlantics were involved. The location is given as Stoats Nest, and although it is clearly winter time, no other information is known.
Wentworth S. Gray/J. H. Price

Upper right:
Emerging into the daylight from Lewes Tunnel, No 37 *Selsey Bill* has charge of an up boat train from Newhaven. *IAL*

Lower right:
Sister engine No 38 *Portland Bill* is seen in very early SR days and possibly a plain black livery. Notice what appears to be a corner support for one of the LBSCR overhead wire electrification gantries in the background. During the time of the overhead electrification, a new building for stock repairs was erected at Peckham Rye on the site of some carriage sidings formerly used to berth loco-hauled stock used on the East London line. Further repair shops were also provided at Selhurst. *IAL*

Upper left:
In early SR days, and displaying Maunsell livery, 'H1' No B41 *Peveril Point* reposes on the turntable at what is believed to be Battersea. *IAL*

Lower left:
'H2' Atlantic No 421 is depicted probably when new on what is likely to be the Crumbles ballast siding at Eastbourne — if this assertion is correct, then the gas works is also nearby. The LBSCR for a time used shingle ballast from this location, while it was also a favoured spot for official locomotive portraits. The frame seen hanging from the footplate was part of the Haslar speed recorder. The largest of the former LBSCR tender engines, the Atlantics were all taken over by the Southern at the Grouping, at which time they were recorded as having a paper financial value of £3,262 each.
SLS collection

Upper right:
Seen here with the coupling hooks hanging rather than secured, No 421 later became No 2421 and was named *South Foreland* as part of an SR publicity department drive to create a better image for travellers on the system. *IAL*

Right:
A driving wheel and part of the motion of *South Foreland* recorded at Newhaven in 1947. *C. C. B. Herbert*

Upper left:

A stunning view of 'H2' No 424, later *Beachy Head*, at Victoria. The engine is in as-built condition, complete with bogie brakes and with the driver apparently attending to his oiling near the Haslar speed recorder. The headcode displayed is of interest and consists of a mixture of both lamps and discs, thus making train identification difficult. It has been impossible so far to determine why such a mixture was sometimes carried. Could it be simply that the tender locomotives did not carry lamp irons on which to place spare lamps — although if this were the case, why are they displayed facing forwards? *SLS collection*

Lower left:

The last days of the Brighton Atlantics were spent on Brighton–Bournemouth and Brighton–Plymouth services. At Bournemouth in August 1955 'H2' No 32426 *St Albans Head* has been turned and awaits departure for Southampton and the east; the engine has just 12 months more in service. *Author's collection*

Above:

Trevose Head in Southern days — the small letter 'B' above the middle digit of the number indicates that it is a Brighton section locomotive. By this time, both Westinghouse and vacuum brakes had been fitted, and the only apparent blemish on the engine is the somewhat bent handrail on the smokebox door. *IAL*

'K' Class 2-6-0s

Above:
One of the redoubtable 'K' class 2-6-0s that first appeared in September 1913. The engine is in its original mechanical condition with a short smokebox, although apparently not in original livery, as it was reported that when first built No 337 ran for a time in a red-oxide livery. It was then apparently painted in the grey seen here until February 1914, after which gloss black was applied. The profile of the cab roof was a feature of the class and later had to be modified by the SR in order to comply with the composite loading gauge on the rest of the SR system. Interestingly, this change was not fully accomplished until the mid-1930s. *SLS collection*

Centre left:
A 'K' class Mogul partly modified by Billinton and with a top feed, the additional plumbing doing nothing to enhance what had previously been the clean outline of the boiler. Notice the massive end to the connecting rod and also the centre-line of the cylinders, on the same axis as the centre of the driven axles. *IAL*

Lower left:
At the Grouping the SR slowly began a process of applying a standard form of numbering, with the engine identification being carried on the tender. Here both SR-style numbering and LBSCR ownership are present; the location is unknown, but is possibly Brighton. *IAL*

Right:
'K' class 2-6-0 No 2352 (formerly LBSCR No 352) is seen at Eastleigh in July 1947, not on the scrap road, but demonstrating the appalling condition of so many locomotives immediately prior to nationalisation — a sorry comparison in appearances compared with a few decades earlier. *A. J. Cook*

Above:
A former LBSCR 'K' class 2-6-0, BR No 32353, passes through Ifield en route for Horsham with the Three Bridges breakdown van on the first day of the big freeze, 27 December 1962. *Brian Haresnape*

Tank Locomotives

'A1'/'E1' 0-6-0Ts

Above:
No 40 *Brighton* was one of the original 'A1' class locomotives. Built at Brighton in 1878, this engine was exhibited at the Paris Exhibition of that year, for which purpose it ran light between Dieppe and Paris. Between 1887 and 1888 No 40 was used by Stroudley for a number of tests involving steam sanding, the fitting of iron tubes and a variable blastpipe, all of which were later removed. In 1902 it was sold for £600 to the Isle of Wight Central Railway, having accrued just over half a million miles in LBSCR service. It survived until 1963, when it was preserved, and has now returned once more to the Isle of Wight as No 11. *IAL*

Above:
At Battersea Park — it has to be — No 39 is correctly stabled in mid-gear, no doubt awaiting work on one of the South London line services. Although undated, the view is probably late 19th century, as witness the wooden brake blocks on the locomotive, and just look at the coach behind… *SLS collection*

No 43 was one of the 'Terriers' that was sold, in this instance in 1925 to the Weston, Clevedon & Portishead Railway for £785. It was eventually numbered No 5 by the GWR in 1940, being scrapped at Swindon in 1954. *IAL*

Below:
No 81 *Beulah* is seen some time prior to 1909, in which year it was placed on the duplicate list as No 681. This engine was also sold, in January 1918, to A. D. Invergordon for use by the Admiralty at Inverness, along with Nos 637 and 683. No 81 later passed to other hands, and its eventual fate is not recorded. This location is likewise not reported, but the view is included as the company names on the poster boards are well worth a careful study — they include LNWR, GNR and GWR. *SLS collection*

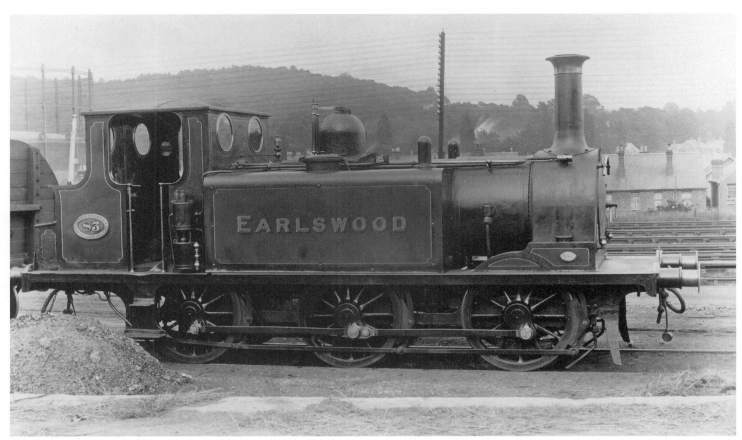

Upper left:
Another engine sold in January 1918 was No 83 *Earlswood*, and to the same organisation as No 81, with the same subsequent history. No 83 is seen here without condensing gear and is fitted with cast-iron brake blocks compared with the original wooden fittings. *SLS collection*

Lower left:
'A1' No 663 stands at an unrecorded location. Just look at that coal — clearly some breaking up is going to be required before it can be used! Notice also that the engine appears to be carrying a wooden number plate, and there is a missing brake block on the centre wheels. *SLS collection*

Right:
The 'E1' class 0-6-0s, built in batches between 1874 and 1883, displayed the distinct family likeness. This is No 11, seen here as it ran between June 1908 and June 1922, when it was allocated to the Locomotive Department. After reverting to capital stock, it survived in service until May 1932. *IAL*

Below:
'E1' No 116 *Touraine* is temporarily stored, judging by the coupling rod across the cab floor. The condition of the side tanks is in contrast to that of the smokebox and chimney, perhaps indicating that the engine has been in the same position for some little time. *IAL*

Upper right:
Picardy, another 'E1' tank, is seen at Battersea. First introduced in the 1870s, withdrawals commenced as early as 1908, but even so some would survive until the 1960s. No 133 was one of those that lasted into BR days, not being condemned until 1952. *IAL*

Lower right:
At Wandsworth Common in 1894, a 24-wagon train is in the charge of 'E1' No 155 *Brenner*. The cameraman has evidently caught the attention of at least one member of the crew, while the fourth vehicle carries an interesting 'W. G. Harris & Co' horse-drawn removal vehicle. *IAL*

Above:
No 120, formerly *Provence*, poses outside what may be the new shed at Eastbourne. As with one of the earlier views, the size of the coal has to be seen to be believed — that coal pick will certainly be needed! — while the cleaners have paid attention not just to the paintwork, but also to all the visible brass. *SLS collection*

Above:
No 129 enjoyed a long life, from October 1878 to June 1957. Originally named *Alençon* — one of a series having French names — the engine is seen at Brighton in LBSCR livery, but in externally poor condition, possibly indicative of the period immediately after 1914. Notice the various hoses for dual braking and steam-heat. *IAL*

Left:
Carrying 'sunshine' lettering, No 2127 — formerly No 127 *Poitiers* — stands at Stewarts Lane. With the absorbtion of the LBSCR into the Southern Railway, the class could now be seen far from its native territory. Indeed, a number of 'E1s', albeit modified somewhat, later found their way to the far reaches of the LSWR west of Exeter, while Southampton Docks was another location where examples were to be found. *IAL*

Above:
Running as Southern No 2156, this 'E1' is fitted with condensing gear — note also the stowage of the coal pick! Injectors were not originally fitted to the class — instead water was delivered to the boiler via two crosshead pumps. A similar fitment existed on certain 'D', 'E' and 'A1X' tank engines, which were so equipped into the 1940s. *IAL*

Above:
A delightful view of another 'Terrier', clearly No 661, on a motor-fitted service on 29 August 1912. Although originally intended to fend off competition from the increasing number of street tramways, the motor-trains operated on routes and branch lines as diverse as Coulsdon–Crystal Palace and the Bognor branch, and even on the coast line east from Portsmouth. Although clearly a better operating system compared with the rods and wires used by the former SECR and LSWR, the LBSCR's compressed air system eventually lost out on the basis of standardisation; however, it is interesting to note that it was eventually resurrected for control use at least, even if vacuum braking eventually became standard. *SLS collection*

Right:
Four 'E1s', Nos 131, 136, 152 and 154, were transferred to the Isle of Wight as Nos W4, W1, W2 and W3 respectively. W3, now named *Ryde*, seen here, was shipped to the island in 1932 and worked there for some 27 years. *IAL*

Left:
Another engine that later migrated to the Isle of Wight in 1932 under the auspices of the Southern Railway was No 152 *Hungary*, which became W2 *Yarmouth*. In earlier days it is seen pausing during what were probably shunting duties at an unknown location, believed to be in the London suburbs. *IAL*

Below:
A 'Terrier' tank on the type of duty for which these locomotives became renowned during their final years, the Hayling Island service. This is No 2661 depicted in 1949, but still in the livery of its pre-nationalisation owner and heading south at the start of its short journey.
Pursey C. Short

'D1' 0-4-2Ts

Right:
'D1' class 0-4-2T No 274 displays a similar appearance to the earlier 'Terrier' 0-6-0T type, but the class was distinguished by larger wheels. Despite this, they had a tractive effort considerably greater than the 'Terriers' due to the fitting of larger cylinders. Built in December 1879, No 274 survived until February 1950. *IAL*

Above:
No 224 *Crowhurst* stands in front of a most interesting background. As has been seen, the names of the various LBSCR engines were predominantly painted on the tank sides — it is not recorded whether there were any complaints from passengers misled as to their intended destination (such confusion is alleged to have occurred on the GWR). *SLS collection*

Above:
No 272 is a non-motor-fitted 'D' tank, but notice that it is equipped with condensing gear. The location is Lewes, and the driver has apparently paused in his efforts at oiling round. The coupling is also correctly stowed as not in use. *R. C. Riley collection*

Above:
No 283 is caught in the act of blowing off steam at Battersea — the wonderful wooden brake blocks will be noted. On top of the side tank can also be seen two lamps, while low on either side of the smokebox are the lubricators. In the background is one of the two roundhouses built here in 1870, which were in use until about 1933 when the remaining locomotive allocation was transferred to Stewarts Lane. *IAL*

Below:
No 230 *Brookhouse* is heading south on passenger duty at Tooting Bec Common, a familiar location for views of LBSCR trains on the move. The route was widened here to four tracks just after the turn of the 19th century. *IAL*

Above:
Clapham Junction was clearly dingy in past times as well as today, not helped of course by countless numbers of steam engines working through. In Southern livery, No 629, with the 'B' prefix above the number, is not far from the location after which it was once named, *Lambeth*. This particular engine survived until January 1936. *IAL*

'D3' 0-4-4Ts

Above:

'D3' 0-4-4T No 391 *Drayton* was probably named after the station illustrated on page 34. In appearance very much a stretched version of the smaller 'D' class, the 'D3s' had a reputation for rough riding when working bunker-first, not helped by the small bogie wheels fitted. *IAL*

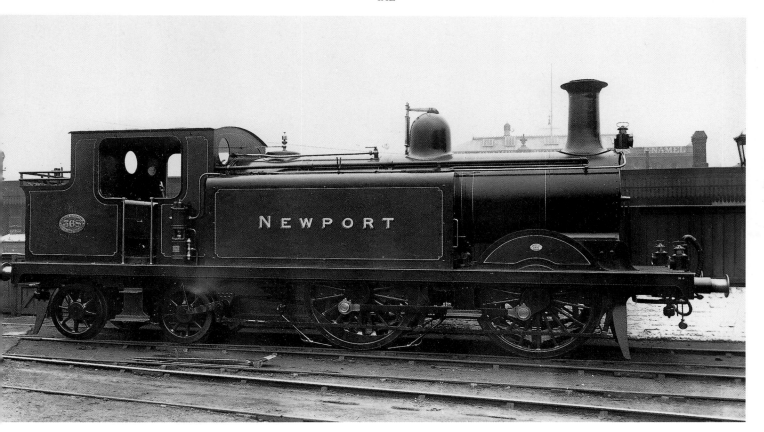

Above:

A wonderful profile portrait of No 368, taken possibly at Croydon. As built, the class had steam sanding gear, but this was not always very successful. Opening cab windows allowed for ventilation or ease of cleaning, while well-fitting side doors minimised draughts. *IAL*

Left:
'D3' No 380 *Thornton Heath* is in full lined livery. A lovely story involving this engine concerns a young cleaner who, on a quiet night at Brighton, climbed up into the cab and probably out of curiosity began to fiddle with the various controls. For some unaccountable reason he then dozed off on the footplate — having left the engine in gear and the regulator open. Fortunately No 380 was very low in steam, but as pressure slowly increased she moved away, coming to rest with a lurch and a bump against another engine, depositing the young man in a heap on the ground. Needless to say, that was the end of his employ by the LBSCR. *IAL*

Above:
'D3' No 388 *Emsworth* is bedecked for the occasion of the Sutton and Norwood Station Masters' and Inspectors' Annual Excursion of 1899. Such embellishment was by no means uncommon for the period, but had been discontinued by the start of World War 1, never to return. *SLS collection*

Upper right:
A striking view of a 'D3X', the nameless No 397 having been rebuilt from a 'D3' in April 1909. The rebuilding involved a replacement boiler and raising the cab slightly, although only limited advantage was gained, and only two of the type were so altered. Interestingly, although both air- and vacuum-braked, the engine is not equipped for steam heating. *IAL*

Lower right:
'D3X' No 397, seen here as SR No 2397, is waiting at Glynde on the coast line east of Lewes. The higher pitch of the boiler and cab is immediately apparent sideways on, and to be honest did little to improve the appearance. *H. C. Casserley*

Left:
Originally known as the 'E-Special' class, the 'E3s' were perhaps better known as the 'Small Radials', and carried names until 1905 when a start was made on repainting them in lined black. The engines were at first employed on suburban passenger services, but later found their true vocation on shunting and transfer good duties. All 16 enjoyed long and useful lives, and apart from one withdrawn in 1949 due to cracked frames, the rest survived until 1956-9, when modern diesel shunting engines took over at the yards where they had formerly shunted. No 170 is seen here in original condition, having been built in 1894. For many years it was to be found working between Tunbridge Wells and Eastbourne, and eventually survived under British Railways until July 1957. *IAL*

'E3', 'E4' and 'E6' 0-6-2Ts

Below:
'E3' No 166 *Cliftonville* is in basically original condition, with its crew and what could also be two cleaners. The wall of coal behind the engine was a common feature at locomotive sheds throughout the country, put down as insurance against any disruption in supplies, but with the stock regularly rotated to prevent it from going 'green' — another job for the cleaners! *IAL*

Right:
No 459 *Warlingham* is also in original condition and carrying Stroudley goods green livery, although the class was used on both passenger and goods working. *IAL*

Below:
The first of the 'Small Radials', 'E3' No 165 *Blatchington*, is on what appears to be a ballast working heading north approaching Dorking. The engine has been fitted with a replacement chimney to the design of Mr B. K. Field, a former North Staffordshire engineer, which henceforth became known as a Marsh chimney. The first 'E3' to be built in November 1894, this was also the last of the type to be withdrawn in November 1959. *IAL*

Upper left:
The larger 'E4'-type tank engines were also known as 'Large Radials', and one, No 473 *Birch Grove*, is preserved on the Bluebell Railway. This particular example is No 485, formerly named *Ashington*, which emerged from Brighton in May 1899. In all, 75 of the class were built between December 1897 and September 1903; 12 were requisitioned for service near the front line in 1917/18, although all later returned to the LBSCR. *IAL*

Lower left:
'E4' No 465, formerly *Hurst Green*, is fitted with a replacement chimney. These engines were popular with both crews and operators, and although used for both passenger and freight, it was on the latter that they were perhaps most successful. Most survived into BR ownership. *IAL*

Above:
Also built for freight working, although with smaller driving wheels than the 'E4' class, the 12 members of the 'E6' class were used initially around the London area; No 412 *Tandridge* is seen here at Norwood. A major change to the last two of the type was to have been the substitution of the rear pony truck with an additional pair of coupled wheels, thus becoming an 0-8-0T. In the event all eventually appeared as seen. They were constructed at Brighton between 1904 and 1905, and the last four never received names. *IAL*

A far larger tank design was the 'I1' 4-4-2T, a wheel arrangement popular among designers at the time, but in reality a considerable waste of adhesive opportunity. Renowned as free-running engines, they needed to be, for as built they were decidedly shy steamers, having a boiler capacity far too small in proportion to their size. Nevertheless the design was used on some prestige workings, as seen here with No 600 decorated for Royal Train duty to Epsom Downs on Derby Day, circa 1907. *IAL*

'I' Class 4-4-2Ts

Below:
No 600 is seen again at Epsom Downs, attached to the five-coach LBSCR Royal Train. This particular set was built to the design of the then CME, R. J. Billinton, and entered service in 1897. The stock was retained exclusively for Royal duties until May 1924, when it was downgraded for use on 'business' trains between Eastbourne and London Bridge. *IAL*

Right:
A much more lowly duty for 'I1' No 3 is hauling gas tanks between Eardley Sidings and Victoria, complete with LBSCR brake-vans at either end. Gas replenishment for carriage lighting was of necessity undertaken outside the terminus at Victoria.
R. C. Riley collection

Below:
Originally intended for use on the prestige services between Brighton and Victoria, the class later migrated to trains running to Tunbridge Wells before cascading again to lesser duties as more modern motive power, then eventual electrification, arrived. Being less flexible in their usage compared with the 0-6-0T or 0-6-2T designs, all would probably have been gone by the 1940s had it not been for the need to maintain as much motive power as possible due to the war effort. Accordingly withdrawals occurred between 1944 and 1951, although none of the engines achieved a million miles in service.
SLS collection

Upper left:
The larger 'I2' 4-4-2Ts were built in 1907/8, and none carried names, No 15 is seen at Epsom Downs on Royal duty prior to World War 1. This was also the real peak time for the class, for with a return to peace in the 1920s larger engines arrived and all the 'I2s' had gone by 1940. The finish on No 15 can only be admired — not a speck of dirt is visible anywhere, and note the whitewashed coal! Notice also the detail of the brake cylinder operating the bogie brakes, and the polished sand pipes. *IAL*

Below left:
Another view of the Royal Race Special, this time en route at Banstead.
Wentworth S. Gray/J. H. Price

Upper right:
No 15 became No 2015 under the Southern Railway, and is seen here coupled to a former SECR 'birdcage' set near Lewes; these engines were banned by the SR from working over former SECR lines in Kent. *Author's collection*

Centre right:
No 2007 was rebuilt with a larger boiler, and reclassified as an 'I1X'. It was recorded at Eastleigh and looks to be fresh from overhaul.
Author's collection

Below:
'I2' No 19 is posed for the official photographer at the head of what was to be the stock for the new 'Southern Belle' service. This prestige service operated on a 60-minute timing between Brighton and London, and with a load restricted to just five vehicles, albeit heavy Pullman cars, it was within the capability of the class. Later, as loadings increased, the train was given over to haulage by the Baltic tanks and 'H1' and 'H2' class Atlantics. The service survived until superseded by the all-electric 'Brighton Belle'.
National Railway Museum, York

Above:
No 22 is a brand-new 'I3', in works grey and fitted with a Haslar speed recorder. All of the 27 'I3s' were constructed at Brighton between 1907 and 1913, with this particular engine reported as having cost £3,418. *SLS collection*

Below:
'I3' No 83 is on what is believed to be a direct service between Brighton and Littlehampton. At least one member of the public is showing a passing interest, while the engine crew appear to have the blower hard open in an attempt to raise some more steam.
R. C. Riley collection

Right:
Large though Marsh's pair of 'J' tanks were, they were not the biggest tank design on the LBSCR, although the use of large 4-6-2 tanks was logical on what were restricted distances for the fastest trains on the LBSCR system. Even so, it was the practice for the engines to turn at the end of each run. No 325 *Abergavenny* is seen at Wivelsfield on a down working in 1910. Interestingly, the livery is grey with black and white lining, with the name and number in white shaded with black. *IAL*

'J' Class 4-6-2Ts

Above:
The other 'J' class 4-6-2T, No 326 *Bessborough*, is seen at the head of what the LBSCR publicity department described as the most luxurious train in the world, the 'Sunny South Express'. However, the passengers would only have had an hour to enjoy such finery between London and the Sussex coast. Clearly a posed view, the locomotive is in works grey, while the Pullman cars are in standard umber and cream. *R. C. Riley collection*

Right:
A wonderfully atmospheric view of the former *Bessborough*, now running as SR No 2326, on the 'Sunny South Express' northbound near Falmer between Lewes and Brighton in 1936.
C. C. B. Herbert

Left:
L. B. Billinton's seven Baltic 4-6-4Ts presented the pinnacle of tank engine design on the LBSCR. Constructed at Brighton in 1914, 1921 and 1922, they remained in service until the mid-1950s, albeit rebuilt by the Southern as tender engines in the mid-1930s. No 329 *Stephenson* was one of three of the type to be named, and is seen running through Hassocks on a Brighton service, complete with indicator shelter. *IAL*

'L' Class 4-6-4T Baltics

Below:
Named in memory of fallen comrades in the Great War, No 333 *Remembrance* is seen at Victoria with temporary Southern insignia prior to full renumbering. *B. E. Thomas*

Locomotive Sheds

Right:
The general dominance of tank engines in Battersea yard, probably around the period 1910/11, is apparent, while it is possible to positively identify three engines by number: Nos 156, 428 and 556. *IAL*

Below:
The old and the new at Battersea during the tenure of Marsh: 'H2' No 422 is coupled to a Stroudley 'G', the latter by now on the duplicate list. Sadly, the background to the print is not totally clear, although it does include a number of gantries for the electrification scheme as well as a fascinating array of coaching stock. *IAL*

Above:
This is the depot at New Cross Gate — or more accurately part of it! This is the 'New Shed', which was constructed some time after 1870, and the locomotive is Stroudley 2-4-0 No 207 *Freshwater*, dating from January 1876; as the brickwork appears little smoke-blackened, it was perhaps photographed not long afterwards — unfortunately the print is undated. No 207 survived in service until February 1901. *IAL*

Upper right:
On a Sunday morning in 1904, the locomotives and stock at Brighton are still and there is apparently not a human in sight! Of the locomotives in view, the following can be identified: 'D3' No 397 *Bexhill*, 'F' No 343 *Wilmington*, 'B1' No 214 *Gladstone*, 'D3' No 378 *Horsted Keynes*, 'A1' No 44 *Fulham*, and another 'D3', No 375 *Glynde*. *IAL*

Lower right:
Horsham shed was once the headquarters of a district that included Three Bridges, Midhurst, Littlehampton and Bognor. However, its importance diminished as its satellite depots closed with the onset of electrification, although it would survive to the end of steam working. *L. J. Catchpole*

Above:
At the other end of the main line, this is Brighton running shed in 1901. The steam crane is stored pending use, while a number of named engines, including *Hungary*, *Fulham*, *St Leonards* and *Cornwall* can be identified. *SLS collection*

Above:
The old part-roundhouse shed at Eastbourne survived until 1911, before being replaced by a straight-road shed. Just one engine is clearly recognisable: 'Terrier' tank No 65 *Tooting*. This particular machine was one of the early casualties, being withdrawn in 1901 in consequence of train weights and speeds overtaking the limited power available from these diminutive engines. *IAL*

Below:
Another view of the old shed at Eastbourne. On view are a variety of engines, but predominantly three 'D1' tanks, Nos 254 *Hambledon*, 362 *Kidbrooke* and 294 *Rosebery*; the latter was later renamed *Falmer* until March 1897. Also visible is 'E6' No 409 *Graffham* and 'E1' No 141 *Mentone*. No doubt those in the bowler hats represent authority. *IAL*

Below:
The locomotive facilities at Portsmouth were of necessity rudimentary as the main depot for the area was but a short distance away at Fratton. Visible are two locomotives: 'B4X' No 2070 and an LSWR 'L12'. The view was clearly taken in SR days, but is not untypical of the varied ownership of locomotives that would have been seen here prior to the grouping, as this section of line was jointly owned by the LBSCR and LSWR. *E. Jackson/R. C. Riley collection*

Rolling Stock

Below:
Part of the interior of the works at Lancing, established as a separate entity for the construction and maintenance of the LBSCR's carriage and wagon stock. The mixture of materials, primarily of course steel and timber, will be noted. The presence of the Pullman vehicle is a slight mystery: certainly the LBSCR was running a Pullman service by the turn of the 19th century, but the Pullman Car Company had its own works at Preston Park at Brighton, so its presence must remain subject to conjecture. *M. G. Joly/R. C. Riley collection*

Upper right:
Four-wheeled passenger brake-van No 102 is reported as having been part of Train Set No 54; notice the solid Mansell wheels and guard's ducket. The ride in such a short-wheelbase vehicle was no doubt lively at speed. *IAL*

Lower right:
Assorted LBSCR and SECR machinery trucks at Eastbourne, carrying containers belonging to the Portsmouth-based removal firm of Curtiss & Sons. *IAL*

Above:
The 'Continental Express' ran between London and Newhaven, and was a direct competitor to the SECR's boat trains to Dover and Folkestone. Included in the formation is a brake-van, four lavatory composites and two ordinary composites, as well as a Pullman. *IAL*

Below:
'Alberta' was a Pullman Parlour Brake seating 31 passengers, and was used on the 'Southern Belle' service. Built by the Metropolitan Amalgamated Railway Carriage & Wagon Company at its Lancaster works, this was one of seven vehicles regularly used on the named train, all carried on six-wheel bogies. *SLS collection*

Signalling

Upper left:
This magnificent gantry controlled the entrance to and exit from Brighton station, recorded at the height of mechanical signalling in the first decades of the 20th century. *IAL*

Above:
These slotted-post signals are on the main line at Selhurst before it was quadrupled. It is therefore possible to date the view to the last years of the 19th century. *IAL*

Left:
New signalling is being installed at what is believed to be the approach to Eastbourne. *IAL*

Upper right:
During strike action in 1912 troops and police were brought in to guard strategically important signalboxes when there was fear of sabotage. What are believed to be Grenadier Guardsmen are on duty at Balham Intermediate box. Apart from verbal intimidation, missiles such as stones and bottles were thrown, although the soldiers did not have the benefit of steel helmets as protection. *IAL*

Lower right:
A typical LBSCR signalbox, and one that has survived in preservation: Horsted Keynes, at the junction of the lines to Lewes and Haywards Heath. The latter route was electrified, hence the warning board placed on the brickwork. *IAL*

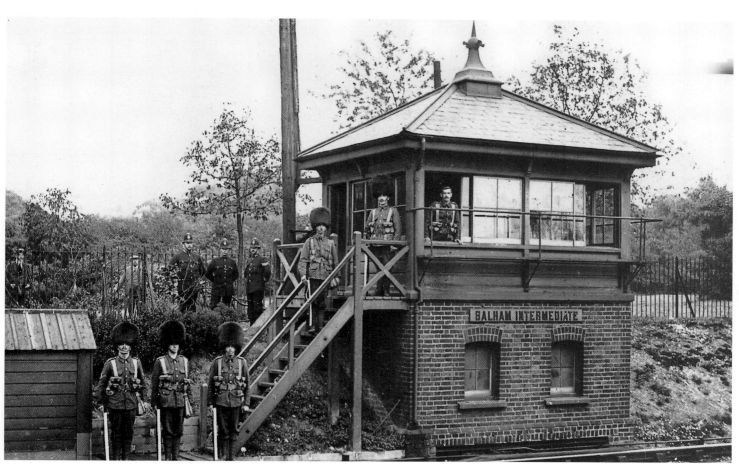

Electrification

Above and left:
Electrification of part of the London suburban system of the LBSCR was completed in 1909, and was an immediate success. It many respects, however, it was ahead of its time in the use of overhead catenary compared with the alternative third rail system. Power was obtained at 6,700 volts AC at 25Hz, and while perhaps at first similar in appearance, there was a marked difference in the technical equipment compared with modern-day overhead electrification. Sadly this non-standard system covered far less route mileage than the third rail used by the LSWR, so after the grouping it was the LBSCR that had to give way. History would none the less prove the LBSCR to have been correct, and the opportunity had been lost to develop a system that in many respects was decades ahead of its time. *IAL*

Above:
This is the approach to the LBSCR station at Victoria following electrification; note that the SECR side on the right is devoid of masts. Mechanical signalling still remains, so the job of the lineman and lampman are not to be envied among the energised wires. *IAL*

Below:
Electrification at Norwood Junction, looking north towards Bromley Junction and Penge. Despite the additional masts and wires, the whole scene is still that of relative neatness, lacking the clutter — and, regrettably, the graffiti — that would later blight the area. *IAL*

Above:
On 9 September 1904 No 239 *Patcham* has become derailed near Cocking while working the 3pm goods train from Midhurst to Singleton. This view records the third and finally successful attempt to re-rail the engine, two previous efforts having seen a chain snap and a crane almost becoming derailed itself. The cause of the accident is not recorded, but at the time it occurred the train was running on plain track. The cranes are from Brighton and New Cross. *IAL*

Accidents

Left:
Some of the wagons from the damaged train. Fortunately the only injury was to the guard who, despite seeing his van smashed to pieces around him, escaped with just cuts and bruises. *IAL*

Above:
Far more serious was the derailment of a Brighton–London express on 29 January 1910. This was caused by a wheel shifting on the axle of a carriage, which unfortunately occurred as the vehicle in question was approaching pointwork at Stoats Nest station. Five people died on the train and two others on the station, in addition to 42 injuries. *IAL*

Left:
'E4' No 515 is in trouble at Norwood Junction in 1911. On this occasion the engine has failed to stop and has lost its chimney in the process.
R. C. Riley collection

Right:
An unfortunate accident occurred at Barcombe Mills in the summer of 1921 when heat spread the tracks. 'D1' No 253 was involved, and personnel from the Civil Engineer's and Chief Mechanical Engineer's department are surveying the damage. *IAL*

Steamers

Above:

In 1862 the LBSCR joined with the French railway company Ouest to operate cross-Channel steamer services. The 1,067grt SS *Arundel*, depicted here, was built at Newhaven in 1900 for the cross-Channel steamer route from Newhaven to Dieppe. She was later used as a troopship during World War 1 before being sold to breakers in Germany in 1934. *IAL*

Below:

The 605grt paddle-steamer PS *Normandy* possibly laid-up at Newaven. She was built by John Elder & Co for the LBSCR in 1882 and later sold to Liverpool & Douglas Steamers. *IAL*

Staff

Above:
Shed staff at Brighton in 1921.
Unfortunately, no names are given.

Right:
On 18 June 1938 the fireman looks out of
the cab of his 'E5X', possibly viewing the
operation of the injector, while working a
Horsham to Dorking push-pull service
between Holmwood and Dorking. The
third rail has been laid, with full
electrification commencing on this section
a few weeks later. *IAL*

Official views of an LBSCR ticket collector, guard and
stationmaster. *IAL*

Miscellany

Above:
An LBSCR cast-iron notice. *SLS collection*

Right:
Unfortunately, the location of this timepiece is not given, but it is included as an example of such items of station furniture that once adorned most of the stopping places owned by the company. As proof of ownership the company initials are of course included. No doubt at the time there was little thought that such an embellishment would place a considerable value on what was then regarded as an everyday item. *IAL*

Below:
An occupation crossing on the main line near Worthing. *IAL*

Left:
What is believed to be a lamp box, photographed in Horley station yard in 1949. *R. C. Riley collection*

Right:
The unique LBSCR Wallis & Steevens 12-ton road roller, No 2565, painted in LBSCR engineers department livery. New on 9 October 1901, it is seen here in Southern days complete with Stroudley 'A1' chimney top and also still retaining its LBSCR owner's plate. It ended its days in Sunderland. *IAL*

Lower right:
A Civil Engineer's inspection vehicle — complete with correct headcode discs! *IAL*

Above:
Everything was labelled! *R. C. Riley collection*

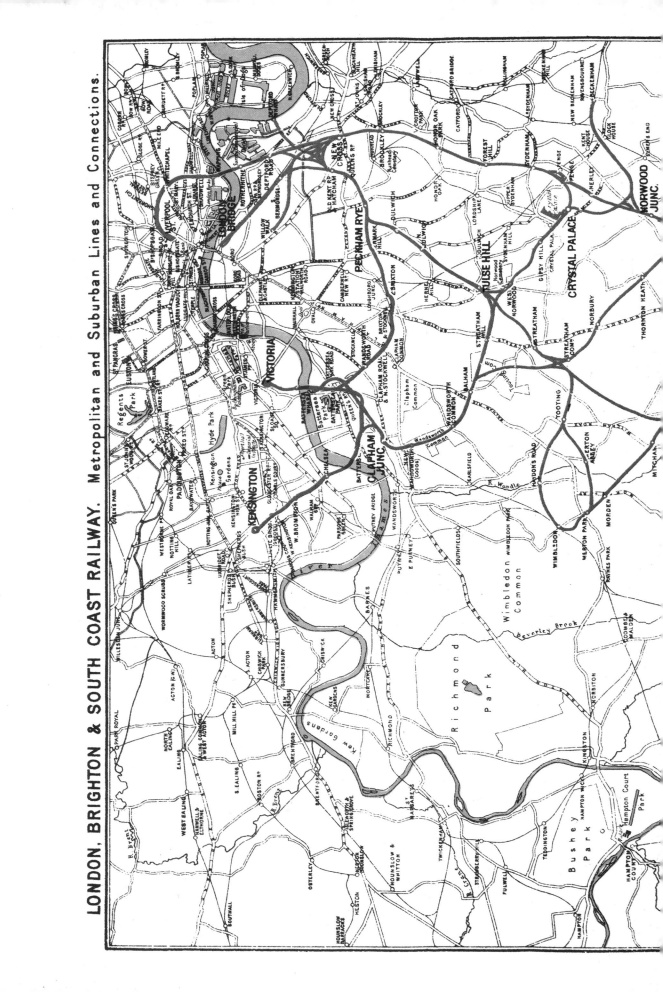

LONDON, BRIGHTON & SOUTH COAST RAILWAY. Metropolitan and Suburban Lines and Connections.